DATE DUE

THINKING BLACK

Also by DeWayne Wickham

Fire at Will
Woodholme

THINKING
BLACK

Some of the Nation's
Best Black Columnists
Speak Their Minds

EDITED BY

DeWayne Wickham

Crown Publishers, Inc.
New York

Published by Crown Publishers, Inc., 201 East 50th Street, New York, New York 10022. Member of the Crown Publishing Group.

Random House, Inc. New York, Toronto, London, Sydney, Auckland

CROWN is a trademark of Crown Publishers, Inc.

Printed in the United States of America

Design by Lenny Henderson

Library of Congress Cataloging-in-Publication Data
Thinking Black : some of the nation's best black columnists speak their minds / edited by DeWayne Wickham.—1st ed.
    1. Afro-Americans—Social conditions. 2. Afro-Americans—Social life and customs. 3. Afro-Americans—Race identity. I. Wickham, DeWayne.
E185.86.T4 1996
305.896'073—dc20   95-34133
                                        CIP

ISBN 0-517-59937-6

10 9 8 7 6 5 4 3 2 1

First Edition

Contents

2

FOREWORD BY PAMELA NEWKIRK 9

INTRODUCTION BY DEWAYNE WICKHAM 17

1: OUR MOTHERS, OURSELVES

Betty DeRamus	Remembering Mama 34	
Lisa Baird	"Ain't I a Woman?" 42	
Brenda Payton	Apple Juice, Ice Cream, and Grapes 50	
Miki Turner	Someday We'll Talk 53	

2: ABOUT BLACK MEN

Dwight Lewis	Where Are the Fathers? 60
Harold Jackson	A Message to Black Men 66
Howard Bryant	The Search for Role Models 80
Claude Lewis	Memories of James Baldwin 86
Claude Lewis	He Led the Way 93
Michael H. Cottman	Dad 99
Dorothy Gilliam	Crossroads to Africa 109

3: GLIMPSES OF THE PAST

Larry Whiteside	Double Duty 116
Howard Bryant	Joe Black's Legacy 125
Jeff Rivers	The Gospel According to Smokey and Curtis 131
Peggy Peterman	Lest We Forget 135
Dwight Lewis	Ed Temple's Tigerbelles 143

4: THE COLOR LINE — AND DEGREES OF BLACKNESS

DeWayne Wickham	*The Color Line*	150
Lisa Baird	*A Churning in My Gut*	159
Betty Bayé	*Let's Talk Black*	163
Michael Paul Williams	*What's in a Name?*	167
Brenda Payton	*Black Like Me*	172
Brenda Payton	*To Be Young, Gifted, and . . .*	178
Jeff Rivers	*White Christmases, Black Santas*	182
Jeff Rivers	*"Joy Spring"*	185
Deborah Mathis	*Ghettocentrism*	188
Derrick Z. Jackson	*The Mark of the Beast*	197

5: THE BALLOT, THE BULLET, AND OTHER ALTERNATIVES

Allegra Bennett	*Black Labels*	210
Allegra Bennett	*Enjoy the Gas*	215
Richard Prince	*The First Amendment Is Not the Enemy*	221
Wiley Hall, 3d	*The Myth of Drug Wealth*	234
Gregory Stanford	*A Crusade for Our Children*	241
Michael Paul Williams	*Substance Over Style*	251
Miki Turner	*The Silence of Athletes*	256
Norman Lockman	*Black and Brazen*	259

PHOTOGRAPH CREDITS   269

THINKING
BLACK

Foreword

Pamela Newkirk

In 1827, just months before slavery was abolished in New York, several prominent African-Americans met in the home of M. Bostin Crummel to explore ways to counteract the overwhelmingly negative depictions of African-Americans in New York City newspapers.

The group decided to fight back by publishing their own newspaper, and without delay *Freedom's Journal* was launched on March 16, 1827, marking the birth of the nation's first African-American newspaper, and of black newspaper commentary.

"We wish to plead our own cause," trumpeted the first editorial. "Too long have others spoken for us. Too long has the public been deceived by misrepresentations, in things which concern us dearly."

It continued: "From the press and the pulpit we have suffered much by being incorrectly represented. . . . Our vices and our degradation are ever arrayed against us, but our virtues are passed by unnoticed. . . ."

The editorial, more than anything, stressed the need for African-Americans to define themselves, a role that today is filled by a rich chorus of African-American columnists employed at daily and weekly newspapers across the nation. *Freedom's Journal*, edited by Rev. Samuel E. Cornish, a Presbyterian minister, and

John Brown Russwurm, one of the first African-Americans to graduate from college in the United States, dedicated itself to fighting slavery and securing full citizenship for blacks. Much of the commentary that has followed in the more than century and a half since has likewise championed the causes of African people across the globe, presenting perspectives otherwise absent from public discourse.

The tradition of black commentary has, at its best, been characterized by selfless acts of courage by African-American journalists who often sacrificed their own comfortable stations in life in their pursuit of justice. Educated and committed to lifting a race from brutality and oppression, these pioneers were as much warriors as writers. During the period following Reconstruction, when blacks were increasingly the victims of segregation, disenfranchisement, and lynchings, *Free Speech*, a local black Memphis newspaper, called attention to the lynchings of eight black men and bluntly challenged accusations that five of them had raped white women.

"Nobody in this section of the country believes the old threadbare lie that negro men rape white women," said the editorial of May 21, 1892, written by twenty-three-year-old editor Ida B. Wells, who was also part owner of the paper.

"If Southern white men are not careful they will over-reach themselves and public sentiment will have a reaction and a conclusion will be reached which will be very damaging to the moral reputation of their women." The gutsy editorial sparked calls for revenge in the local press by writers who were apparently unaware that Wells was a woman.

"Patience under such circumstances is not a virtue," read the editorial in *The Evening Scimitar*, on May 25, 1892. "If the negroes themselves do not apply the remedy without delay it will be the duty of those whom he has attacked to tie the wretch who utters these calumnies to a stake at the intersection of Main and Madison Sts., brand him in the forehead with a hot iron and perform upon him a surgical operation with a pair of tailor's shears."

Said another editorial in the city's *Daily Commercial* the same day: "The fact that a black scoundrel is allowed to live and utter such loathsome and repulsive calumnies is a volume of evidence as to the wonderful patience of Southern whites. But we have had enough of it. There are some things that the Southern white will not tolerate, and the obscene intimidations of the foregoing have brought the writer to the outermost limit of public patience. We hope we have said enough."

Indeed they had. A mob destroyed the office and print shop of *Free Speech* and Wells was exiled from the South. The former teacher, who hailed from Mississippi, first went to New York where she lectured against lynchings and published her first pamphlet, "Southern Horrors," which carefully documented them. The editorial that spelled the newspaper's doom was also printed in the pamphlet, as was a letter from Frederick Douglass to Wells, dated October 25, 1892. "Brave woman! you have done your people and mine a service which can neither be weighed nor measured," Douglass wrote.

Speaking for African-Americans has never been easy. The editors of *Freedom's Journal* learned this when they found themselves embroiled in an internal debate on the merits of colonization, a movement to send African-Americans back to Africa. Senior editor Cornish was adamantly opposed to colonization, while Russwurm was torn. The colonization issue was an emotional and divisive one among African-Americans and may have contributed to Cornish's decision to resign from the paper after only a few months at its helm. By the end of 1828, with Russwurm the newspaper's sole editor, *Freedom's Journal* editorials moved from staunchly against colonization to neutral, weighing both sides of the issue. Finally, in 1829, Russwurm sparked a controversy when he openly supported colonization and was forced to resign as editor. The journalist ventured off to Liberia to join the budding African-American colony there, and published the *Liberia Herald*. He never returned to the United States.

Freedom's Journal folded that year, but was followed by a succession of other African-American newspapers, among them *The Rights of All* in 1829, and *The Weekly Advocate* and *The Colored American* (for which Cornish for a time served as editor) in 1837. As black newspapers flourished, so too did the public demand for racial equality. An August 25, 1884, editorial in the progressive

Cleveland Gazette was characteristic of the irreverent tone of newspaper editorials of the day. The editorial declared that Ohio's 25,000 African-Americans were united in their appeal for a black representative to be sent to the National Republican Convention.

The editorial warned against taking the demand lightly and chided "the contemptuous manner with which some of our white friends hasten over our columns: and we wish to remark, while we have the floor, that our little sheets voice the wishes of our people, and exert an influence that cannot be obtained any other way. Need we say more?"

By the turn of the century, African-American columnists were well known for their social and political commentary. The journalist who perhaps most embodied the militancy of African-American commentary of the day was William Monroe Trotter, who launched *The Guardian* in Boston on November 6, 1901. Trotter, a Harvard College graduate born to privilege, nonetheless forfeited a life of affluence to give voice to the misery of his race. Trotter attended protest meetings throughout the country and was a vocal critic of Booker T. Washington and his call for black accommodation.

The Guardian was renowned among African-American journals of the day for Trotter's blistering page 4 editorials, which castigated U.S. presidents, foreign leaders, and African-Americans, most notably Washington, whom Trotter believed ill served the race. Week after week Trotter assailed Washington, the nation's most prominent African-American, who advised former slaves to be patient in their quest for equal citizenship and to pursue industrial education over more intellectual fields.

Trotter's unrelenting attacks aside, Washington, a key dispenser of Republican Party patronage, enjoyed wide support from African-American newspapers, many of which liberally published his news releases while benefiting from his financial contributions. But Trotter's assaults did not go unchallenged by Washington, who heavily subsidized *The Colored Citizen* and *Alexander's Magazine*, two rivals of *The Guardian*. Neither newspaper survived and Trotter's attacks continued unabated.

"The northern Negro has no rights Booker Washington is

bound to respect," he wrote in one editorial. "He must be stopped." In an editorial on July 26, 1902, Trotter directed some of his fury at African-American leaders who had attended a national meeting convened by Washington:

"The silence of the Afro-American Council at its national meeting at St. Paul on President Roosevelt's policy of appointments to office in the South is one of the most culpable derelictions of that body. This policy has been a flagrant fault of the new administration and the race looked to this organization as practically the only national organization it had which was formed to guard its political interests to voice its protests against this ignoring of the Negro in appointments. The failure of the council to do this was therefore a betrayal of trust."

Of Washington, he warned, "The Negro people will see the more clearly the need of repudiating Booker T. Washington as a leader." That same year, in a September 13th editorial, the solitary nature of Trotter's battle was evident:

"How long, O Booker, will you abuse our patience? How long do you think your scheming will escape us? To what end will your vaulting ambition hurl itself. Does not the fear of future hate and execration, does not the sacred rights and hopes of a suffering race, in no wise move you? The colored people see and understand you and they know that you have marked their very freedom for destruction, and yet, and yet, they endure you almost without murmur! O times, O evil days, upon which we have fallen!"

On October 22, 1904, some six decades before the civil rights movement took shape, Trotter wrote: "The policy of compromise has failed. The policy of resistance and aggression deserves a trial."

On July 10, 1905, Trotter was among the thirty blacks at a historic meeting at the Erie Beach Hotel in Ontario, Canada, to form what came to be known as the Niagara Movement. Spearheaded by Trotter's former Harvard schoolmate W. E. B. Du Bois, who over the years Trotter had criticized for his neutrality on Washington, the group's meeting was the first collective campaign for full citizenship by African-Americans in the twentieth century. Du Bois and Trotter headed the group's Press and Public Opinion committee and together drafted the group's "Declaration of Principles," which read like a direct challenge to Washington's leadership:

"We refuse to allow the impression to remain that the Negro-American assents to inferiority, is submissive under oppression and apologetic before insults. Through helplessness we may submit, but the voice of protest of ten million Americans must never cease to assail the ears of their fellows, so long as America is unjust."

The declaration was pure Trotter—uncompromising, defiant, and direct. It continued:

"The Negro race in America, stolen, ravished and degraded, struggling up through difficulties and oppression, needs sympathy and receives criticism, needs help and is given hindrance, needs protection and is given mob violence, needs justice and is given charity, needs leadership and is given cowardice and apology, needs bread and is given a stone. This nation will never stand justified before God until these things are changed."

The new civil rights group was incorporated in January 1906. By then Du Bois, whose book *The Souls of Black Folk* had been widely and critically acclaimed, had begun to secure his place as the nation's most important commentator on issues concerning African people. Du Bois clearly understood the power of the press. In an attempt to reach a wider audience and circumvent Washington's considerable sway on the press, Du Bois invested in a printing plant in Memphis and published *The Moon Illustrated Weekly*, which made its debut December 2, 1905. The *Moon* was out of business by the following August, and in January 1907, Du Bois published a new monthly, *The Horizon: A Journal of the Color Line*, which was more widely circulated than his first venture. The *Horizon* covered a wide array of topics, from lynchings in the South, to national politics and developments in Africa and Asia. From its pages, in 1908, Du Bois urged African-Americans to abandon the Republican Party, which he said had taken them for granted.

But Du Bois would find his greatest forum with the debut in November 1910 of *The Crisis*. As director of publicity and research for the National Association for the Advancement of Colored People, Du Bois founded and edited for twenty-four years the monthly magazine that became this century's most influential journal of African-American protest. While billed as the organ of the NAACP, the magazine under Du Bois became his own personal platform. With his trademark irreverence, he unflinchingly railed against the black clergy, the black press, and white paternalism, along the way straining relations with some of the organization's board members and benefactors, many of whom were white philanthropists.

But Du Bois relished the coming of age of black self-determination and advocated it at all cost. "Instead of being led and defended by others, as in the past, American Negroes are gaining their own voices, their own ideals," he wrote in his book *The Negro*, published in 1915. "Self-realization is thus coming . . . to another of the world's great races."

Just as Du Bois's militancy had often created turmoil at the National Association for the Advancement of Colored People, so too did Trotter's cost *The Guardian* financial support, while sapping him of his personal real estate fortune. But while he and his newspaper struggled financially, he continued to reject advertising for liquor or products that he believed denigrated African beauty, such as skin-bleaching creams. By 1913, Trotter was forced to sell his home and other personal property to keep *The Guardian* afloat.

"Principle robs it much of money," he wrote a friend in 1913. "Yet I would rather have people criticize my poverty than get money against my principles."

In 1919, Trotter worked his way to Europe as a second cook on a European freighter in order to attend the International Peace Conference in France. There, he gave speeches criticizing President Woodrow Wilson's proposal to form a League of Nations, which would unite all white men and nations, and exclude people of African ancestry.

In 1926, during a meeting with President Calvin Coolidge, Trotter presented him with a petition signed by 40,000 people demanding the total end to legal racial discrimination. Eight years later, on his sixty-second birthday, Trotter, by then destitute and partially blind, walked to the roof of the apartment building where he rented a room and fell to his death. Fortunately his spirit, and that of Du Bois, Russwurm, Wells, and others, prevails, as demonstrated by the commentaries that appear on the pages that follow.

These contemporary writers, all part of a lineage steeped in principle and protest, have taken up the mantle during a period when America and its relationship to African-Americans is more complex than ever. Unlike their forerunners, they largely write for white-owned publications, typically for primarily white audiences. But like their forebears, they must often swim upstream, against powerful currents, to define and uplift a people in crisis, a race that is still, near the close of the twentieth century, misrepresented or ignored around the world. It is left to them to amplify the voices in the wilderness.

Pamela Newkirk
Assistant Professor,
New York University,
Department of
Journalism and
Mass Communication

Introduction

DeWayne Wickham

The Negro leader of today is not free," H. L. Mencken complained in 1929. "He must look to white men for his very existence, and in consequence he has to waste a lot of his energy trying to think white. What the Negroes need is leaders who can and will think black."

This was a surprisingly candid observation from Mencken, a white columnist whose iconoclastic views left little room for such sentiment. Mencken's words were meant to prod African-Americans loose from the social, political, and economic tethers that in his day so tightly bound them to white America. Over the years, some of these shackles have been loosened, if not broken. Black elected officials—local, state, and national—who were as novel as sideshow freaks in the first half of this century, now number in the thousands.

In the 1992 election alone, the number of blacks in Congress grew by 50 percent—and that year for the first time a black woman was elected to the United States Senate. In Mencken's day there were but a handful of truly wealthy African-Americans. Today, even in the face of widespread black poverty, black folks can be counted among this nation's super-rich.

These are all impressive gains.

But something is missing. No people have ever come to really know themselves and their place in time if they were without voice. Every generation of white Americans has had an intellectual conscience; a prodding, rallying voice to champion their causes and decry their failures. Over time, many white newspaper columnists—like Mencken, Joseph Alsop, Walter Lippmann, A. J. Liebling, Mary McGrory, Pat Buchanan, Erma Bombeck, Mike Royko, Dave Barry, William Safire, and Ellen Goodman—have assumed this role.

It was Liebling who once said that in America no one enjoys freedom of the press except those who own one. He could have also added, "Or those who are given license by newspaper editors to speak their mind."

It is into this latter category that columnists fall.

Many of today's white columnists are well known and widely read. A good number of them have authored books and become television commentators as well, thus expanding the reach of their voice. But until recently there were precious few black columnists working for daily newspapers—and only one, Carl Rowan, with anything that approached the notoriety and celebrity that leading white columnists enjoy. Slowly others have begun to come forth. Clarence Page, of the *Chicago Tribune,* won the 1989 Pulitzer Prize for commentary. *Washington Post* columnist William Raspberry did the same in 1994. But for the most part, black columnists have practiced their craft in relative obscurity.

There is a small, but growing, number of black columnists working in journalism today who are trying to give voice to the many joys and pains of black America. For the most part they write for just a single newspaper, mostly in urban settings east of the Mississippi. Many of these black voices are muffled by their lack of access to a broader audience of readers. This anthology offers them a chance to be heard—and to have their thoughts considered—beyond the confining limits of their newspaper's circulation.

The original essays that appear in this volume are the work of some of the nation's most thoughtful and provocative black columnists. Many of them lack household names, but they all write with the verve and clarity of those who do. They are, in fact, just what Mencken ordered: black columnists who can and do "think black."

But thinking black does not necessarily mean thinking alike. As you will soon see, the commentary on these pages reflects the fairly broad range of interests and opinions that exist among African-Americans. For instance, in her essay about the effects ideological labels have on African-Americans, Allegra Bennett writes:

"Black folks must undergo a radical change in the way we think about ourselves as a race—no longer as the victims of 130 years ago who are owed something, but rather as extraordinary survivors who take life's lemons and make the tastiest lemonade in the neighborhood. We are in no position to do that when others are out there reenforcing the belief that someone else owes us the juice squeezer, the pitcher, and the sugar."

While Bennett's voice lacks the shrillness of the black professional conservatives who cross-dress as journalists, she is no less committed to the core values of their ideology. Betty Bayé, on the other hand, has planted her feet squarely to the left of center when it comes to the race question. In her essay, Bayé grapples with the gnawing issue of how to take black folks to task in her column without giving white critics the ammunition they need to bring down the race.

"White columnists can criticize bad, ignorant white people all day long because bad white people, no matter how ignorant, no matter how terrible their crimes, still are perceived as individuals," she writes.

"Bad, ignorant black people, on the other hand, are not perceived as individuals, but as representatives of the race. The irony, of course, is that good black people are generally perceived as individual exceptions to the race."

And then there's Norman Lockman, whose irreverent, Afrocentric piece on being brazenly black straddles the gulf between the ideological right and left:

"Every time I hear of a white colleague being bemused—and often deeply troubled—over why black people clump up together in cafeterias, college dormitories, even neighborhoods, I am reminded how difficult it is to explain in America the phenomenon of feeling OK about being black without apology.

"It is no laughing matter in America to be black and to be willing, even momentarily, to publicly reject white standards and conventional wisdom. We all know that those who do are marginalized and, if possible, humiliated. It may be preferable to the whippings and death penalties for black brazenness in slavery time, but can nevertheless be a terrifying prospect."

But if this book were just a collection of polemic essays, it would do little to showcase the great range of interests—and the writing ability—of the black columnists who have contributed to its pages. Fortunately, it is much more than that.

It is about black history—Joe Black and the Negro baseball league in which he once played. It's a tribute to writer James Baldwin and journalist Robert Maynard. And a soulful remembrance of singers Smokey Robinson and Curtis Mayfield. It is a book about daughters and their mothers; a collection of essays about black men and their fathers. It is all of this and much, much more.

It is the rhythmic, introspective essay of Lisa Baird, whose light complexion and straight hair causes her to ponder what it means to be a black woman. This hauntingly self-revealing work probes the soft underbelly of black America's internal racial conflict.

"I am in junior high, wearing my dashiki, wrapping African fabric around my head. A copy of *Seize the Time*, *Soul on Ice*, or *The Autobiography of Malcolm X* is firmly tucked under my arm," she reminisces.

"My evenings are spent washing my hair in detergent. Girl swore to me Tide would make your hair nappy. Wetting it down and winding it tight into dozens of pin curls; picking them out in the morning. I've got my 'fro. But is it a 'natural' if you have to worry about it going flat if you sweat?" Baird wonders plaintively.

Equally powerful is Betty DeRamus's essay about her two mothers: the one who raised her that she struggled to know and the one who gave birth to her that she never really knew.

And then there are the black men in this book who raise their voices in the name of black manhood. Harold Jackson contributes an essay in which he uses the story of A. G. Gaston, a black Alabama businessman who struggled against the odds to become a multimillionaire, to encourage today's young black men to bend but not break under the pressures of a changing world.

Dwight Lewis wonders in print "where are the fathers," as he struggles to understand what has driven so many black men from the home.

Michael Cottman knew his father. His dad never strayed far from home, at least not without his wife and son in tow. Cottman writes about the special relationship he has with his father and the many life experiences they shared. His story is a much needed reminder that most black fathers are loving, caring, supportive men who give unselfishly of themselves to their families—an essay that is both simple and compelling in its richness.

In addition to giving readers access to these exceptional black voices, this anthology serves another important purpose. It preserves for all time the meaningful contributions African-Americans made to the public discourse during an important period in American history—a time when they themselves have become an endangered species.

Increasingly, black columnists have come under fire at the very newspapers that employ them. Privately many complain of being pressured to tone down their opinion in an apparent concession to the growing political muscle of conservatives. A few, like New York *Daily News* columnist Earl Caldwell and Curtis Austin, of the *Dallas Morning News*, had disputes with their editors that cost them their jobs.

Others, like Derrick Jackson, of the *Boston Globe*, and Wayne Dawkins, of the *Camden* (New Jersey) *Courier Post*, needed an outpouring of public support to keep their columns from being downgraded, or lost altogether.

But the most egregious case of all is that of Lisa Baird, a columnist with *The Record*, of Bergen County, New Jersey, who resigned in 1993 shortly after her editor refused to publish one of her columns.

The column in question dealt with a December 1993 shooting

on a Long Island Rail Road train that resulted in the deaths of six passengers—all but one of them white—and the wounding of many others. The person who was arrested and eventually convicted of the crime was Colin Ferguson, a black man of Jamaican birth.

In her column, Baird decried the gut-wrenching feeling she believes many African-Americans experience each time a black person is accused of committing such a high-profile crime.

"You see, black people can't just mourn the loss of life or denounce the crime," she wrote. "This society does not allow us that level of humanity. We also have to deal with the fallout, and the double standards and contradictions that fallout reveals."

The column was rejected by a white editor who said in a memo to Baird: "Today's column demands that I spend appropriate time as the editor arguing with you intellectually. I frankly disagree with some [of your] premises."

Baird was also reminded that inasmuch as her column usually ran on the front page of the local section of the newspaper—and not the editorial page—it should rely more on the opinions of others, rather than on her thinking. The column, he wrote, should "percolate from the real world, not your intellect."

The day before Baird's unpublished piece was to have run, Mike Kelly, a white male columnist at the newspaper wrote a column that appeared on the front of the local news section. In it, he bemoaned the fact that an automatic pistol with a fifteen-bullet clip, like the one Ferguson used in the train shooting, could be legally purchased in this country. Nowhere in his column did Kelly quote any sources for his piece. It did not "percolate from the real world," but clearly was born of his intellect.

Like Baird's column, the piece Kelly wrote was chock-full of opinion. Unlike hers, his found its way into the newspaper.

Thinking Black is no remedy for such a lopsided, single-minded approach to journalism. It is, however, an answer to all such crude attempts to silence a black voice of dissent. Lisa Baird deserved better, and in this anthology she is given the voice her editor at *The Record* sought to silence. The column he suppressed appears in chapter 4.

Baird, like every other contributor to this important work, was encouraged to go beyond the limits, structural or otherwise, imposed upon them by the newspapers that employ them to explore any issue of their choosing.

What appears on the following pages is not only the product of that work effort, but also a testament to the wisdom of Mencken's call for African-American "leaders who can and will think black."

In chapter 1, four columnists contribute poignant and soul-searching essays about their relationship with the maternal figures in their lives. Mothers, grandmothers, and stepmothers, all have a special place of reverence among African-Americans. They are the glue that holds black families together—the straw that stirs the drink in black life.

Betty DeRamus, of the *Detroit News*, writes about the two mothers in her life and the man whose love they shared. It is a riveting commentary that seems to spring as much from August Wilson's *Fences*, as it does from her own life experiences.

DeRamus, an award-winning journalist who has visited and reported on fourteen African countries, became a columnist in 1987. Her work has often placed her at the cutting edge of history, as in 1990 when she went to South Africa's Victor Verster prison to witness the release of Nelson Mandela. The columns she wrote about that occasion won her a Best of Gannett Award.

Lisa Baird's career as a columnist with *The Record* of Bergen County, New Jersey, lasted just eighteen months. She began her twice-weekly column in July 1992, and abruptly ended it in December 1993. Before that she worked for newspapers in Miami, Indianapolis, and Westchester County, New York. She is currently an associate metropolitan editor at the *New York Post* and occasionally writes free-lance columns.

Her essay echoes the question that black abolitionist and women's rights activist Sojourner Truth asked in her now-famous 1851 speech, "And a'n't I a woman?" In it she demanded that poor black women, too, be given all the rights and dignity afforded white women of her day.

Baird's essay strikes a more contemporary chord. A woman of

light complexion with straight hair, she struggled to affirm her blackness and to connect with her heritage in ways that are seldom talked about outside the confines of black America. The title of her essay is, "And Ain't I a Woman?" But the question she actually raises is, "And Ain't I a Black Woman, Too?"

For the past twelve years, **Brenda Payton** has written a column three times a week for the *Oakland Tribune*. She is also a commentator on public radio. Payton has worked for newspapers in New Bedford, Boston, and San Francisco.

In the first of three essays she contributed to this anthology, Payton writes a short but moving piece about her 108-year-old grandmother and the sacrifices she's made in life.

Miki Turner became the first black woman to write a regular sports column for a major daily newspaper in 1989 when she worked for the *Oakland Tribune*. Currently a sports columnist for the *Orange County Register*, in Santa Ana, California, Turner has also worked as a broadcast journalist in Boston, New York, Washington, Oakland, and Los Angeles.

Her contribution to this chapter is an open letter to her mother that is a passionate confession of her failings in their trouble-filled relationship. It is also a fond and affectionate remembrance of someone who Turner has never been able to thank for all that she's done for her—until now.

In this chapter titled "Our Mothers, Ourselves," these four essays combine to paint a revealing picture of the black woman's continuing struggle to shed the scar tissue that centuries of degradation and abuse have produced.

In chapter 2, six writers turn their attention to that long endangered human species: the black male. Their essays range from a criticism of absent fathers to a fond look back at two black men who never strayed far from their roots.

Dwight Lewis is a columnist with *The Tennessean*, of Nashville, Tennessee. A recipient of the 1994 National Association of Black Journalists award for outstanding commentary, Lewis has been writing a column since July 1993.

The essay he has contributed to this chapter, one of two by him in this book, grows out of his own fatherly involvement in the life of his son. It is an attachment that has had Lewis racing from work to coach Little League baseball and Junior Pro basketball teams his son played on and making regular visits to the school he attended. It was while doing the latter that he chanced upon the subject of the essay that's titled "Where Are the Fathers?"

In 1991, as an editorial writer and columnist for the *Birmingham News*, **Harold Jackson** won the Pulitzer Prize for editorial writing. That same year he was named Journalist of the Year by the National Association of Black Journalists. Currently an editorial writer for the *Sun*, of Baltimore, Jackson started writing columns in 1987.

His essay, "A Message to Black Men," is an appeal to young black men not to be unbending, but instead to find a way to adapt to their circumstances in order to survive. It's a controversial message that is rooted in the teachings of Booker T. Washington and the success of one of his disciples, millionaire businessman A. G. Gaston.

Howard Bryant, a graduate of Temple University's school of communications and theater, began his journalism career at the *Oakland Tribune* in 1991 as a sports writer and columnist. Three years later, he entered the "Information Superhighway" as a reporter and columnist for the paper's Sunday technology section.

A chance assignment—to go into Oakland's ghetto to find a role model for black youngsters—was the impetus for his essay. In it, Bryant views his quest as a wasted effort. A better strategy for dealing with the problems that plague inner-city neighborhoods, he contends, is to mount a frontal attack on the maladies that afflict the black underclass, not offer its members some mystical figure in the hope of staunching their misery.

Claude Lewis's long and distinguished journalism career has taken him to jobs with *Newsweek*, the *New York Herald Tribune*, the *Philadelphia Bulletin*, and a stint as founding editor and publisher of the *National Leader*, a now-defunct weekly black newspaper that had a national circulation. He has served as both a Pulitzer Prize juror and member of the Tony awards committee.

His work has taken him all across this country and to nations on four continents. And it has brought him in contact with some of the true legends of our times—two of whom he writes about in his contribution to this anthology.

Michael H. Cottman writes about his father with the love and admiration of a son who never wanted for a dad, in a time when far too many do. His essay takes us on a journey that an increasing number of black boys never get to make—a trip through life at his father's side. He tells us about his dad's love for jazz, his unquenchable thirst for black literature and the many lessons his father taught him. Most of all, he reminds us of the forgotten truth that most black men are good and loving fathers.

A reporter and contributing columnist with *New York Newsday* until it closed in 1995, Cottman also has worked for the *Atlanta Journal and Constitution* and the *Miami Herald*. He was a member of a team of *Newsday* reporters that won the 1992 Pulitzer Prize for spot news. Cottman is currently writing a book about the discovery of the *Henrietta Marie*, a slave ship that sank off the coast of Key West, Florida, in 1700.

Since 1979, **Dorothy Gilliam** has been a columnist with the *Washington Post*. A member of the National Association of Black Journalists Hall of Fame, she served as the group's president from 1993 to 1995. She has also chaired the board of directors of the Institute for Journalism Education.

In her contribution to this anthology, Gilliam takes us along with her to the African motherland on a spiritual and cultural awakening trip that provides her with a ringside seat to one of black Africa's important historical events. It is a journey that brings an uplifting end to this chapter, aptly titled "About Black Men."

In chapter 3, five columnists write with great longing about some of the people and places they don't want us to forget. If, as has been often said, journalism is the first rough draft of history, then their inclusion in this anthology should go a long way toward preserving our memory of those they have written about.

When **Larry Whiteside** began his journalism career in 1959, Dwight Eisenhower was in the White House and the civil rights movement was barely in second gear. A native of Chicago, he grew up during the time when the "color line" divided black and white baseball players. Instead of sitting in "Watermelon Heaven"—the bleacher seats set aside for black fans in Comiskey Park, home of the Chicago White Sox—Whiteside went elsewhere to see the Negro League baseball teams play.

In his essay, Whiteside talks about the times he spent watching some of the great black ball players of that era—like Monte Irvin, Goose Tatum, and Josh Gibson—play the game the major leagues reserved for whites. The stories he tells are a simple but revealing account of a time long past that should never be forgotten.

Howard Bryant, in the second of his two essays, picks up where Larry Whiteside drops off. He writes about Joe Black, one of the Negro League stars who followed Jackie Robinson across baseball's color line. The first black pitcher to win a game in a World Series, Black suffered many of the racial slurs and insults that Robinson weathered, but got little of the praise that was bestowed upon Major League Baseball's first black player.

Jeff Rivers takes us back to the days of romance. A time when black women were almost always treated like ladies by black men. Back to the days when the songs that moved black folks to dance and romance came mostly from the soul music mills of Memphis, Detroit, and Philadelphia. All the way back to the time when Smokey Robinson and Curtis Mayfield sang their beautiful love songs.

It's a time he hopes we can somehow recapture.

Rivers's journalism career has landed him jobs with the *Memphis Commercial Appeal* and *Ebony* magazine. He was an administrator with the Institute for Journalism Education before joining the *Hartford Courant* in 1989. Presently, he is an associate editor and columnist at the Connecticut newspaper.

Peggy Peterman is a columnist and editorial writer with the *St. Petersburg Times* who has spent more than three decades with the Florida newspaper. In 1989, she received the National Association of Black Journalists Lifetime Achievement Award, the highest honor bestowed by the nation's largest organization of minority journalists.

In her contribution to this book, Peterman remembers the courage and spirit of the elders of her childhood in Tuskegee,

Alabama, and bemoans the failure of many who have come after them to carry forth those important qualities.

Her essay is a haunting reminder of what we once were, and an inspirational example of what black folks must again become to save the race from mass destruction.

In the chapter's last essay, **Dwight Lewis** shares with us his recollections of Ed Temple, the legendary coach of Tennessee State University's equally legendary Tigerbelles—an all-female track team that, over time, sent forty of its members to the Olympics. Like the other works in this chapter, this one, too, gives readers a glimpse of black America's glorious past.

Eight columnists tackle the divisive issue of "The Color Line" in chapter 4. Four of them contributed to earlier chapters of this book; four others make their first appearance in this volume.

In the title essay, **DeWayne Wickham** looks at the racial turmoil of the twentieth century and predicts more of the same in the next millennium. But worse, he foresees in the coming century a replay of the racial violence that's marked the past hundred years.

Since 1985, Wickham has been a columnist for the Gannett News Service and *USA Today*. A founding member and former president of the National Association of Black Journalists, he also has worked for the *Richmond Times-Dispatch*, *U.S. News & World Report*, the *Sun*, of Baltimore, and *Black Enterprise* magazine. His syndicated column appears in newspapers from Vermont to Hawaii. In 1987, Wickham won the National Association of Black Journalists' award for commentary.

Lisa Baird's second contribution to this book is the column that her editor at *The Record* refused to print. It is a candid response to a senseless act of violence committed by a black gunman against a train full of suburban commuters, nearly all of whom were white.

In her essay, **Betty Bayé** tackles the question that haunts many black columnists: How do you take to task someone black who is deserving of a public scolding without giving aid and comfort to black folks' enemies? It is a difficult question for which she offers a fairly simple answer.

Bayé started in journalism as a reporter for the *Daily Argus,* of Mount Vernon, New York. In 1984, she joined the staff of the *Louisville Courier Journal.* A former vice president of the National Association of Black Journalists, she became a columnist in 1991.

Michael Paul Williams weighs in with the first of two short essays that he contributed to this book. Here, he enters the debate over what the descendants of former slaves should be called, and poses the question: How can we figure out where we're going if we can't decide who we are?

Williams joined the *Richmond Times-Dispatch* in 1982 and became a columnist ten years later. His commentary has been praised by the Virginia Press Association and panned by *Richmond* magazine, which labeled him the "Local Newspaper Columnist Who Makes You Want to Tear Up the Paper." He takes pride in both.

Brenda Payton, whose first essay is in chapter 1, contributes back-to-back pieces in this chapter. The first takes on the troubling issue of the racial divisions among blacks, the hierarchy of skin color among African-Americans that some jokingly call the "brown paper bag test." She says we'll never heal the wounds of slavery if we don't first get over our own color hangups.

In her final submission, Payton joins Williams in trying to unravel the mysteries of the ever-changing names that people of African descent in this country want to be called.

Jeff Rivers, whose work first appears in chapter 3, also contributes back-to-back essays in this chapter. In the first, he takes an interesting look at multiculturalism—and our continuing struggle with racial identity—by questioning the race of Santa Claus. It is a gentle treatment of a very explosive issue. In the last of his three short essays, Rivers talks about what it's like—both literally and figuratively—to be called a "nigger." Enuf said.

Before **Deborah Mathis** became a White House correspondent for the Gannett News Service, she worked both in broadcast journalism and as a reporter for various newspapers. In 1988, she became a local columnist for the *Arkansas Gazette.* Her column was syndicated by Tribune Media in 1992.

Mathis writes about the intraracial factionalism that tears at the tattered seams of black America. In her essay, she questions the "provincial standard of ghettocentrism" that hangs over our search for the authentic black and concludes that "every black experience is the real thing."

Derrick Z. Jackson rounds out the chapter with an essay that warns that African-Americans run the risk of entering the next century branded with the mark of the beast. It is a cogent exploration of the blame game, which, he believes, puts black bigotry under greater scrutiny than that of whites.

Jackson has been a columnist with the *Boston Globe* since 1988. Prior to joining the *Globe*, he worked for *Newsday*. He has twice won the National Association of Black Journalists' award for commentary.

The final chapter of this anthology is an eclectic collection of essays that fit neatly under the broad title, "The Ballot, the Bullet, and Other Alternatives." The first is **Allegra Bennett**'s defense of those blacks who defy "the limitations of political branding"—people who, she says, "challenge the status quo of ideas."

Her second contribution is about the escalating urban holocaust that spares no one, not even young children, from its merciless violence. It is a stinging reminder of the moral decay that is engulfing our cities and her strong belief that "some killers need to be executed."

Bennett is an editorial writer and occasional columnist for *The Washington Times*. She also has worked for the *Sun*, of Baltimore, and for Spectrum New York, a news service she helped found in New York City shortly after graduating from college in 1974.

From Prince Whipple, the black man who crossed the Delaware River with George Washington, to the bawdry music of the rap group 2 Live Crew, **Richard Prince** says the First Amendment has proven to be a friend, not the enemy, of African-Americans. He traces a path through history that is full of examples of how this constitutional amendment has been used to the benefit of black people. It is an eye-opening trip that might cause some blacks to pause before reacting the next time they have an encounter with offensive speech.

Prince began his journalism career at the *Newark* (New Jersey)

Star-Ledger. He has worked for the *Washington Post* and the *Rochester Democrat and Chronicle,* and the *Rochester Times-Union,* where he was both an editorial writer and columnist. A former editor of the *National Association of Black Journalists Journal,* Prince currently writes a column called "Journal-isms" for that publication.

Wiley Hall, 3d wrote a twice-weekly column for the *Evening Sun,* of Baltimore, that was also distributed nationally by the Los Angeles Times News Service. The paper ceased publishing last year. Hall is the recipient of more than three dozen journalism awards.

A writer whose columns focused largely on how public policy affects people on an everyday basis, Hall's essay attempts to debunk the myths he says many young blacks have about the good life drug traffickers live. He argues that it is these myths—and not reality—that give drug dealers their appeal with the young people who wrongly covet their lifestyles.

Gregory Stanford, too, writes about his concern for black children. He calls for a national crusade to save black children from the social decay and racial oppression that continue to threaten their survival. In his essay, he lays out a strategy for the crusade he says is needed to rescue black children from a cycle of self-destruction.

Stanford is an editorial writer and columnist for the *Milwaukee Journal Sentinel.* A 1993 winner of the National Headliner award for commentary, he is also the recipient of the 1990 Richard S. Davis Award, the highest honor given to writers at the Milwaukee newspaper.

In the last of his two essays in this anthology, **Michael Paul Williams** writes about how former Virginia governor L. Douglas Wilder's fall from grace was the by-product of the unwieldy balancing act that came with "being a black governor in a predominantly white state."

Miki Turner, who also appears in chapter 1, contributes a cutting-edge essay to this chapter about how many of today's athletes have remained silent in the face of the racism that still pervades every aspect of American life. What she has to say is short and to the point.

Norman Lockman is a columnist and associate editor for the

News Journal, of Wilmington, Delaware. He has also worked for the *Boston Globe,* where in 1984 he was a member of a team of six reporters that won a Pulitzer Prize for special local reporting.

"It is not easy to be black without apology in America—or anywhere else in the world where we are thought of as inferior beings. But learning to be black without apology is the threshold of true freedom," he writes in the closing essay of this anthology.

And H. L. Mencken might add, it is a prerequisite for every African-American "who can and will think black."

1
Our Mothers, Ourselves

Betty DeRamus

DETROIT NEWS

Remembering Mama

My mother tried to strangle me on my twenty-first birthday after I stumbled home with champagne on my breath. It was the first time I'd ever drank, and the wine must have made me taste rainbows, smell stars, or start a conversation with the moon: I began singing in my room, awaking Mama. However, I tumbled back down to earth fast when I felt her hands squeezing my throat as she begged me to quiet down. She didn't want the neighbors to think I'd become a drunk.

It's truly a miracle that I'm alive. But America's towns and cities are crammed with "miracle children." We're the flowers that pushed their way through the cracks in the pavement; we're the grass that grew at the edge of the desert. We became teachers, talk-show hosts, and writers despite being tossed into trash cans or tortured. My miracle was surviving being abandoned by two mothers—one sane, one sometimes insane—with the help of a soft-talking father with a spine of steel.

But this isn't only my story. It's the story of Leila Amy, who slept on a plastic cot in an attic until she was six years old, tearing cornflakes into crumbs to make them last longer. It's the story of Benny, whose mother pulled the shades whenever the family ran out of food and made her children sit in darkness, glowing with hunger, tormented by memories of oatmeal. It's the story of anyone who has had to slip inside her own soul to find the strength to live.

I was my daddy's out-of-wedlock child by a woman who lived near my father and his wife in Tuscaloosa, Alabama. My birth mother's name was Mattie Will Nesby, but I was a grown woman with strands of gray before anyone told me about her—and backed up the claim with proof. She died in childbirth or shortly afterward, leaving me with relatives who couldn't afford another squalling, hungry mouth. At the time I was born, Mattie had one other child, but I don't know whether it was a girl or boy or how old. When my father heard I was missing meals and moaning for my absent mother, he scooped me up and took me home to his sweet-faced little wife—a woman with a temper twice her size, a woman who had attacked one of my father's girlfriends with an ax.

I don't know how Daddy found the courage to do what he did. Perhaps it was because he knew Mama couldn't have children herself. Two or three times she'd tried raising some of her brother's children, polishing them up and putting them in green suits and dresses that looked like lemon layer cakes. Sooner or later, though, someone always came for them. Then my father showed up with a child he had fathered by another woman. It must have stuck a knife through Mama's heart, realizing another woman gave him a baby. But at some level, it might have pleased her, too. She finally had a child no one could snatch away. She finally had a rope that would tie my father to her.

They left Alabama when I was just a few months old and moved to Detroit, a city crammed with people who slammed cars together all day and played card games, bid whist and tonk, all weekend. Though Daddy had only an eighth-grade education, he managed to get a skilled job by passing a test designed for college graduates. We lived on Mack Avenue, a street where worn-out frame houses leaned against each other like friendly drunks. Just a block away was Hastings Street, with its black-owned dry cleaners and drugstores, supermarkets and nightclubs, hotels and movie theaters, spicy barbecue joints and shoeshine stands. Prostitutes took customers into hallways, under porch steps, or even in wheelbarrows. Preachers without churches put up tents on vacant lots and prayed until the rising sun sat them down.

In Detroit, they created an identity for me without bothering with any paperwork. I should have suspected something when I discovered I had no birth certificate and that my mama often forgot my birthday. A buzzer should have sounded in my head when I wrote off for a birth certificate and received one for Betty Jean Nesby, a name I now know was truly mine. Yet I grew up believing I was the daughter of Lucille Richardson from Eutaw, Alabama, and Jim Louis DeRamus from Autauga County, Alabama, even though that was only half-true. I was my father's daughter, all right—I had his slanted eyes, his slightly stooped shoulders, his broad wall of a forehead. Yet some part of me must have also resembled that unknown mother, Mattie Nesby from Monroe County, Mississippi. As I grew older, that part of me— that secret blood—made mama hate as well as love me.

No, I wasn't beaten with bed slats or slammed with shoes or even slapped. My parents seemed determined to shower me with everything they'd missed. I attended Catholic schools, where I learned to answer questions with worried whispers and walk in straight lines. A piano teacher named Mr. Bolden came to my house and played boogie-woogie as long as my father kept his beer glass full and foaming. In fact, I sometimes felt so embarrassed to be eating pork chops while my friends gulped bread and catsup that I'd give things away. I still remember the spanking I got after removing a box of fresh donuts from our refrigerator and giving them to a family of twelve. Eventually, we did have some tight times, especially when my father's asthma forced him to go on disability. We even took in borders for a while, including an old East Indian man, who'd rap on the floor with his cane and declare, "When you dead you done." But through all of this I cannot remember ever going to bed hungry. I only remember misery.

Mama bubbled over with complaints, her pot of simmering sorrows always hot. She complained about having to work and complained about my father's other women, a charge I never believed for a second. She shook with fury because her sister,

Minnie, who lived next door to us, had been able to play while Mama worked. Most of all, as I grew older, she complained about me.

"Betty isn't pretty like me," she would announce to any playmates who came to see me. If I tried to learn how to cook or clean, she'd snatch the iron, broom, or mop from my hands and say, "That's all right. I can do it better." Later, she would tell me I was lazy, ungrateful for her sacrifices, and completely incapable of caring for myself out in the world—the kind of child who'd return with spoiled milk if you sent her to the store for ice cream. I tried once to ride a bike with some cousins in Cleveland and scraped my knee. She immediately made me stop, telling me I couldn't do it. The same thing went for roller-skating. To this day, I cannot ride a bike or skate and had to be hypnotized before I could drive a car.

Don't get me wrong. I don't blame Mama for any of this— not now. She had thirsted for an education, but as the oldest girl in her family, she'd been forced to stay at home and change her brothers' and sisters' diapers. At the age of eight, she was standing on a stool so she could wash dishes and iron clothes for neighbors. She had been beaten so severely as a child that her personality shattered into two different people, one all-loving, one twisted by hate. At fifteen, she ran off to marry my dad, a handsome man ten years her senior. I'm sure she was hoping for both love and a little luxury, but what she got was a husband who worked on the railroad all week and swigged corn whiskey with his buddies on the weekend while she, sober as a locked door, stayed at home and stewed. No wonder she kept telling me to go to school so I wouldn't have to depend on a man. No wonder she couldn't stand to see an iron in my hands. No wonder she was smothering me with fried chicken and chocolate-covered love one minute and trying to choke me the next.

As a child I resented my father's failure to defend me from my mother's rages, which could last all night. I felt betrayed when he told me, year after year, "Your mother's goin' through the change of life." But now I understand. What could he have said? His affair had robbed him of his power, stripped him of his right to silence my mother. He was, however, man enough to take the consequences, to swallow his bitter medicine without breaking the bottle or even making a face. In fact, he was a model father, reading me Bible stories every night, showing me how to sail through storms by creating a calm island in my mind. His example helped me survive, and so did the books I'd bring home from the library—not to mention the John Coltrane and Miles Davis records I played around the clock. The web of music I spun around myself—those tender trumpets, those searching saxophones, those pounding pianos—would sometimes silence my mother, drown her out. "Betty plays the *best* of music," I heard her brag to a friend one day.

I was twenty-three when I finally left home, not knowing how to cook or clean or even make up a bed. Daddy had died the year before, living just long enough to see me strut across an auditorium stage and pick up my college diploma. I stayed home for another year because my mother seemed so stunned by my father's death, so cut off, so lost, I feared she would fall apart if I wasn't there. I even turned down an advertising job in New York —the city where I thought I'd learn how to fight back and talk fast—so I could watch over Mama.

When I finally left home, I did it like a sneak thief. I dumped all my belongings in the backseat of a Volkswagen while my mother was away and moved in with a co-worker. But leaving home didn't really change my life all that much because I took home with me. I chose a roommate who was offended if I wanted to spend a couple of hours alone and silent in my room. I chose girlfriends who would keep me on the telephone until the sun rose, listening to their list of complaints, soaking up their problems, swimming in their doubts and despair. I chose boyfriends who were both needy and easy to leave, no competition at all for Mama. Keeping her out of the mental health system was my mission in life, not getting married.

Her paranoid episodes got worse over time. She would call me at my office and scream and rant for an hour. I would put down the telephone and go about my business, while she continued to talk. Later, she began refusing to leave the house except to see her doctor. She was convinced that if she left, even for five minutes, someone would sneak in to steal a pot, a table, a photograph. She even accused a moving company of switching all her furniture, taking her pieces and replacing them with stuff that wasn't quite the same. After I paid the bills and brought groceries to her apartment, she'd try to pay me for my services, often throwing money down the hallway as I walked away. "I'm your daughter," I'd protest. "You don't have to pay me." She would always bite her lips and look away, never saying the words that must have marched through her mind.

I still remember how she looked the day she finally decided to stop keeping the secret that had poisoned her life and tell me how I'd become her daughter. At that moment, she was no longer a woman who drifted in and out of states of paranoia and personalities. She was the woman who'd worked most of her life, sick or well, smiling or sobbing. She told me she wanted to take me back to Alabama and find some of my birth mother's relatives and show them who I'd become. She said she wanted them to see that she was a real mother, whether or not she'd given birth. She said she wanted them to understand that you don't pass out children like puppies. I wept that day, because for the first time I knew for sure I'd managed to make her proud. I also wept because I'd been freed of the fear that I, too, would lose my mind.

My mother believed I owed everything I became to her, and, in many ways, she was right. She taught me how to create my own world by telling constant stories about people from her past —the cousin who'd served her cold biscuits and saved the bacon for her pastor; the brother who'd shoved his wife down the stairs, knocking out her teeth and good sense; the aunt who decided she really loved women after having eight kids; the sister who hit the numbers on a visit to Detroit and walked around with $12,000 in a brown paper bag. When I was around twelve, I began writing down her stories and making up stories of my own. Putting words on paper became a safe way of managing my pain. I also believe that trying to understand my mother's suffering caused me to develop compassion, a love for the underdog, the disturbed, the hungry, the tossed aside. However, I owe just as much to Daddy, a long-legged whisper of a man, too good-looking for his own good, who couldn't bear to leave his baby behind.

Despite the strange twists and turns of my life, I've made out pretty well in the world. I'm a columnist for the *Detroit News*, a daily newspaper. When Nelson Mandela stepped out of prison in 1990, I was there in that sweaty, shouting South African crowd, taking notes and trying to avoid getting trampled. I also got a chance to see the ancient, unwashed face of the Soviet Union before it cracked into a dozen dangerous pieces. I have a whole wall of framed writing prizes. First prize from the Overseas Press Club of America for writing about hunger in Africa. First prize for a commentary from the Education Writers Association for a column about my old elementary school. Two Best of Gannett prizes for assorted pieces about Detroit's troubles and triumphs. I was even a finalist for the Pulitzer Prize for commentary in 1993, mostly for writing about the Los Angeles riot.

All the same, there's a part of me that would give anything to know what my father saw in Mattie and how much of her lives on in me. Do I have her chin, her cheeks, or her chest? Did she go to bed with books and records, too, or was she just a girl with wide hips and a wink who caught my father's eye? Am I really a "miracle child," a surprising survivor, or is every human life just as strange and sweet?

Lisa Baird

NEW YORK POST

"Ain't I a Woman?"

And ain't I a woman?

She is back. The woman-child with the constant silent plea for the embrace of unconditional love. This little stranger who wants nothing more than to fit in. That little waif who stands just inside the shadows, hoping the world will see and give her what she needs but is too meek to ask. So she wants me to do it for her.

In all these years, few people have paid much attention as she stood there, my constant companion, peering wide-eyed with hope that I would call her out and let everyone see her. Some have gotten a good glimpse at her, many may have sensed she was there. Could it be they know her plea is a siren's call that might lure them into a place where they risk madness from the endless echo of her doubts?

Do they dare not face a colored girl who has considered suicide? She's a heartbreaker, this little too-grown waif. Living with her is not easy. Keeping her hidden has been less threatening than sharing her.

And ain't I a woman?

It had been years since that plaintive and defiant cry of a

race of women denied their beauty and femininity had screamed through my head.

That plea had been mine. The words had pulsed through my blood, swirled in my bone marrow, beaten in my heart so many times. So many times.

And ain't I a woman?

But the poet's words that meant so much to me were not thrust at the world on my behalf. The ears those words were aimed at were white ears; my cry was meant to fall on black ears.

From me these words stayed unspoken. I swallowed them, hard, till I had forced them back from the tip of my tongue and down my throat, down to some place where only the unquestioning love I know black folks can give would find them, far enough down so that the sounds would be muffled so that on most days the deafening roar wouldn't send me hurtling off some high and deadly place. Finally, there were a few moments of peace when I heard them no more.

And now here they are, pounding again inside my head. And ain't I a woman?

The question, this time, is directed at myself. Answering it honestly, changing my life to give meaning to the answer may mean exposing that most tender spot I've kept so well shielded. The reward is great. Is the risk greater? Can I face the truth if I ask:

And ain't I a woman?

The question creeps into my head as I listen to a group of black women, my peers, my sisters—women with whom I share so much, women from whom I've always felt so distant.

They speak from anger, frustration. They are telling the men in the group, black men, that there are problems between us.

The conversation began with one of the women throwing out for discussion her observation of our previous session. She had seen this dynamic: the voices of three black men drowning out the voice of a black woman speaking in defense of a black man.

I began to frown. The other woman chimed in. The brothers, it seems, had been disrespectful of the women as professionals. When the women spoke, they were cut off, ignored. The men were impatient with their opinions. The men did not "piggyback" on points made by the women. The women were not taken seriously.

Puzzled, I replayed the scene. But I didn't see what these women saw.

One sister raised the idea of fundamental differences between us, as males and females. In preparation for our gathering, we had been asked to send copies of our best work.

The sister said she knew the program had been designed by men from the choice of the word *best*. It indicated a competitiveness not natural to women. We would have requested the writer's "favorite" submissions.

I found it ridiculous.

One woman got into a heated exchange with one of the men. He had described one of our member's works as "brilliant"; she told him how much she needed that kind of affirmation of her work from him.

I turned in confusion to the man next to me. He and I were clearly of like minds on the whole discussion—confused as to what brought it on.

I spoke up, and found myself alone, separate and apart from my sisters. Once again.

The debate moved from the room to inside me. It didn't matter if the women were right or wrong; what mattered was that I didn't identify, not one bit, with anything they were saying. What mattered was that I wasn't sure enough of myself—as a woman—to disagree with them more forcefully.

And ain't I a woman.

I am five years old and I'm sitting in kindergarten, gazing at Debbie's long blond hair. I am a child telling my mother I'm glad I'm not brown like her. Scoffing at her words, "You're going to wish you were chocolate like me someday."

I'm in Tricie's dining room.

Eyes squinted against the smoke from the cigarette clenched in her teeth, Tricie's mother expertly holds a parted patch of the girl's hair in one hand and reaches back with the other, retrieving the hot comb balanced atop the flame from the gas jet that had to be lit with a match.

The other girls, Cathy, Vicky, maybe Connie, or Pam, are

there. They will get their hair pressed, too, if not today, some other time. All little black girls do.

Not me.

I am in junior high, wearing my dashiki, wrapping African fabric around my head. A copy of *Seize the Time, Soul on Ice,* or *The Autobiography of Malcolm X* is firmly tucked under my arm.

My evenings are spent washing my hair in detergent. Girl swore to me Tide would make your hair nappy. Wetting it down and winding it tight into dozens of pin curls; picking them out in the morning. I've got my 'fro.

But is it a "natural" if you have to worry about it going flat if you sweat? I am a total revolutionary, down with the brother, firmly against the establishment and the pigs. It is 1968–1969, and as soon as I escape from my bourgeois Negro family I will join the Black Panthers and bring power to the people.

The waif has the nerve to ask if all of this proves I'm black or makes me look ridiculous?

The boys chase me, say I'm fine. The girls chase me, say, "Oh, you think you cute 'cause you light-skin and got straight hair. Somebody needs to kick your ass for you."

My sisters. Black is Beautiful.

What am I?

Am I fine because I'm fine or is it because I look white?

I am reading *Essence*, the magazine for black women. I study its pages, the women on the cover, on the inside, in the ads. Photo after photo: black women, the blacker the better; hair short, natural, nappy.

Some are beautiful, some are plain. Some are tall, some short. Skinny, plump. Young, old.

None are me.

Page after page of beauty tips: makeup for darker skin, styling for "natural" hair, relaxed hair. Product after product for black women.

Nothing for me.

Feature articles, short stories, poetry. Memories of Down South, of bare brown feet on dusty roads, of a grandmother's hands working the soil. Memories of Up North, the projects, the ghetto. Nothing about middle-class high-yella girls like me in *Essence*.

I understand. Really I do. *Essence* is correcting an injustice. It is putting on display all those black women who didn't look like Lena Horne, or me, and telling them, and the world, behold this beautiful black womanhood. It is answering a resounding YES! to the question, And ain't I a woman?

My dark sisters rejoice in *Essence*, and I rejoice for them. *Essence* celebrates black women in all of their glory. But *Essence* does not celebrate me.

It leaves me a little bit lonely. It leaves me with my silent question.

So does Wimp.

On summer days in Sag Harbor he photographs us on the beach, and on summer nights we gather at his house to watch the slides projected on the wall.

Wimp is serious about his art. He shoots portraits of black women.

He does not take pictures of me. I sit in the darkened room watching the photos on the wall—the women are unposed, makeup-free, and they are breathtaking; the pictures capture not just their beauty but Wimp's reverence. To him, they are queens. The brothers who chase tail and hit on me all day and night say I'm fine. But my picture is not there.

I want to scream at Wimp's wall, And ain't I a woman?

Malcolm hated his light skin and red hair, talked of his mother's hatred for her white father, blamed some of that for the demons that stole his mother's mind.

Hating your skin can do that to you.

Then I became a columnist. And the proof that I had been black all along wrote itself across my computer screen. The proof that though some unknown white ancestor had done a hell of a number on the surface, they were not able to bleach my soul.

Black people call me, write to me, to say thank you. Thank you for keeping our issues on the front burner; for speaking our truth, venting our rage, shouting our joy, crying our tears, believing in all that we are. Older black men ask if they can kiss my cheek and older black women don't bother to ask, they just grab hold of me with soft brown arms like my grandmother used to. They call me "child" and speak of how proud they are, and one man had someone pass along a résumé in case I ever needed him because he thought I was a "righteous sister."

And the waif who whispers self-doubt and screams her plea that they return her black love fell silent for a moment.

The little waif in the shadows loved them, even though sometimes it hurt. When they played, she wondered if the reason she couldn't get the rhythm of jumping double-Dutch, wasn't even allowed to turn the ropes, was because, as someone said, "You're double-handed." Or was it because she wasn't black enough?

She, who loved them even when they didn't know how much it hurt that they always wanted to play with her long straight hair —it was like having a life-size doll, the ones with the "natural" hair said—but they took no interest in corn-rowing it.

She, who loved them even through the pain of having her best friend tell her about the time her mother made her walk down the dirt road from their summer house in Sag Harbor to mine while she protested having to make friends with "that little white girl."

She, who loved them while hating her mother every time the folks got together for loudly calling on her to join in and dance, to loosen up and move it, because it made her wonder if she couldn't relax and dance the way other black people seemed to was because she wasn't black enough.

She, who cried out while I kept quiet when my little nephew, overhearing her complain about white people, looked dead at me and said, "You white." She who had spent all those years silently pleading with black people just to see her wholly as one of them and stop the teasing.

The sad little waif who was kept locked in a basement closet where no one would hear her tiny plaints, because the woman she dwelled in could not face the risk of rejection by asking someone to say they understood.

Then the woman began to write. And the people said, "You truly are ours. We love you." And her family said, "Your granny would be so proud." Granny was always proud of me, but this was something much more. She was Enid C. Baird, executive secretary to three of the last four heads of the National Urban League, and she was an honest-to-God natural black woman and she was fierce and classy, and to know that she would be proud of my work for the race is what counts.

And I do know that. The waif shut up all on her own; I thought she was gone.

Then the women started to talk.

I look at these women in the room. This one is light-brown, with a mane of braids. This one is ebony-brown; another light but with dreads; yet another dark, with dreads and truly African features. I wonder if these sisters are truly focused on their womanhood because they never had to give much thought to being black.

But then comes the woman's voice, asking, While you were working so hard to be sure you were a black person did you neglect to check on yourself as a black woman?

I suppose she was there all along. I suppose she cried in her basement dungeon every time I compromised, every time I let someone hurt me, sacrificed my self-esteem, my self-respect because I need to be liked, wanted to be loved.

I suppose she was there every time I let some man treat me badly. She must have been there, must have been the reason I wondered why these men always seemed to treat me with less respect than they showed darker women. Why I held on long after I knew it was no good.

Damn. I hadn't put her to rest, I only muted her for a minute. She was there, sure enough, every time I made a fool of myself trying so hard to fit in.

And now I'm scared. Because this time the woman-child waif is not crying out to the world, she's talking to me. This time, if I'm lonely, if I feel left out, there is no one to blame but me.

It had all been just a prelude. I thought the waif's voice had gone away because I had grown up, but I haven't. I'm still a child, a creation still in progress. The little too-grown girl is still there, asking, daring me to answer. And ain't I a woman.

Brenda Payton

OAKLAND TRIBUNE

Apple Juice, Ice Cream, and Grapes

I'm writing this on the eve of my grandmother's 108th birthday. I would never write, "My grandmother will be 108 tomorrow." Years ago she trained her children, grandchildren, great-grandchildren, and great-great-grandchildren not to take even a day of her life for granted.

She is in great shape, healthy, agile, and strong. Sometimes she seems confused. But I've come to understand it's not a matter of confusion, but of priority. Most of the things we find so pressing and compelling just don't make much difference in her 108-year-old scheme of things. For example, one day she couldn't remember which one of her sons is my father. "What difference does it make whose daughter you are? I know you love me and I love you."

Every time I see her she says something that is a revelation about living, age, love. It's always simple. Usually one or two straightforward sentences. But her words alter the way I've looked at something I thought I understood, redefine something I thought I knew. And usually she says something that cracks me up.

Taking a cue from grandmother, life's pleasures are simple. She loves apple juice, ice cream, and grapes, which she eats while sitting up in bed, supported by the strength of her own back. She doesn't have the patience to fool with propping pillows behind her back for support or waiting for someone to help her scoot back to lean against the headboard. She sits up on her own.

Which is a metaphor for her life. She sat and stood up on her own.

Working her way through college from a sharecropper's background (a phase of her family history she has never talked about), waiting ten years to marry while her husband-to-be put his brothers and sisters through school, raising three sons who grew up to be medical doctors, going back to school where she was the first black student to earn a diploma and where she had to sit outside of the classroom to hear lectures because the school would not allow her to take a seat inside.

She stood up on her own. Always. And somehow the harshness and humiliation of what she endured never seemed to penetrate. Education was her shield. By some force and purity of spirit, she remained unscathed, able to truly understand that racism was the other guy's problem, not hers.

Our heated debates must seem like children's games to her. The issues of color or of our ever changing names are not important enough to attract her attention. Her life speaks for what is meaningful, her strength and her unflagging optimism. Her simplicity. Apple juice, ice cream, and grapes.

Miki Turner

ORANGE COUNTY REGISTER

Someday We'll Talk

I have often found it much easier to walk into a locker room full of naked men than to *talk* with my own mother.

By virtue of my profession, locker room excursions are required suffering. But I don't get paid to *talk* to my mother. So I don't. It's been more years than I can remember since we've pursued anything beyond superficial conversation.

Consequently, I suffer this painful relationship less gladly. I consider it one of my greatest failures. Something I'm more afraid to commit to than my thirty-year mortgage.

Yet, each of us tries in our own way to express our love, but most times the demons at work to keep us apart win. The intimacy enjoyed by many mothers and daughters is foreign to us.

I seldom tell her how nice she looks. Or how courageous I thought her battle against colon cancer—and her ability to deal with its aftermath—was. I don't tell her how miserable I am living in a city where your worth is measured by the labels in your underwear.

I wish I could. How hard could it be?

I don't tell her when I think she's overdosed on the Fashion Fair. Or that her memory lapses and clumsiness probably stem from the drugs she injects daily to remain alive and the radiation treatments she underwent to save her life, rather than old age or some incurable disease.

Maybe she knows that.

I haven't told her that her thirtysomething daughter met this really great guy on the cruise she and my dad subsidized, knowing that would have made her quite happy. Or that I too hate this gap between my teeth that she paid hundreds of dollars to fix when I was a teen. Or how annoying it is to wage war on adult acne. Or why I don't laugh at some of her jokes.

She doesn't have a clue.

I've never told her how much I appreciate the fact that she didn't stop loving me at fifteen when I got caught shoplifting in downtown Cincinnati. Or when I flunked Earth Science in ninth grade. Or when I accidentally broke her favorite casserole dish and lied about it.

I'm real sorry.

I didn't let on how truly painful my friend Chip's death was. Or how I had insomnia for nights afterward because my bed felt like a coffin. I didn't even send the poignant column I wrote about it. If I had, then she would have had to assume the role of mother and I would have had to play the child.

Again.

But, there's no turning back now.

The sins of the mother are always much harder to forgive and forget. For it is taught, it is believed, that mothers are infallible. Incapable of making wrong decisions—errant judgments.

I know this is not true. My mom's made lots of mistakes.

In the past she has done things that humiliated me. Like the time she came to my high school business class and publicly cursed me out for skipping my morning classes.

Busted.

She has embarrassed me. Like the time she took a switch to my hind parts in front of my playmates after I wandered down the street without permission.

My mom has always liked to perform in front of audiences.

She has hurt me. Like the time she threw away all my Jackson Five pictures without remorse. By making fun of my looks and belittling my accomplishments in front of family and friends. Telling them I would never amount to anything. That I was foolish to dream. That there was something wrong with me.

I almost believed her.

And I bet she doesn't realize that she's actually responsible for starting my writing career. I started writing to ease the pain after she chided me when I tried, but failed, to make the teen board of a local department store.

That was a good mistake.

These memories linger, as I am sure they do in her. Because everything bad she's done to me, I've done back. Two-fold. I've never been "Mommy's perfect angel." I was more interested in playing hoops and drawing pictures of imaginary "perfect" families than prancing around in lavender and lace and arching my eyebrows.

I still am.

But at least now I understand what went wrong. Our relationship went awry due to a chemical imbalance. Menopause and puberty. We didn't have a chance after that. We went from being mother and daughter to Big Bitch and Little Bitch.

My hope is someday we'll get past this. That we'll be featured in one of those mother-daughter profiles in *Essence* magazine. Two beautiful mahogany-colored African-American women dressed to a T with serious coifs and flawless makeup.

Then some talented journalist could write about the time my mom surprised me with my first kitten. Or how she used to bundle me up at some ungodly hour in the morning, take me on her job and let me sleep on the bed she made for me out of cardboard boxes until it was time to go to school.

That's love.

Or how she made sure I always had the best clothes from the best stores, while she shopped at rummage sales. How she took me to Sunday School and church every week, so that I would grow strong in the Lord. Or how she slept with me when I had the chicken pox.

That's love, too.

Or how she and my dad nearly mortgaged their future so that I could travel to the places I read and dreamed about. How she worked two jobs, so that I, who barely made it out of high school, could go to Hampton Institute and find myself.

Or how she held me and dried my tears when I had to put my puppy to sleep. How she allowed me—unemployed and unmotivated—to live in her house rent-free for a year, while I tried to find myself again.

Or how she spoils me with expensive clothes and makes all my Christmases very merry. And still makes the best pinto beans on the planet.

That's my mom.

Per usual, the good outweighs the bad. I wonder if she feels the same way.

I wonder if she's a happy woman, having gone through so much in her lifetime. Having overcome poverty and suffered through a less than ideal relationship with her own mother. I wonder why she married my dad and how they met. I wonder how come she never knew her dad.

I wonder what she could have become if she hadn't had to quit school in the eighth grade to go clean some white woman's house. It must have been tortuous for her listening to her friends talk about the Emancipation Proclamation, while she had to give up her right for an education during the New Deal.

I wonder what her dreams were. Are.

I wonder how much it really hurt her that her mother lacked genuine affection for her. But maybe they dealt with that when my grandmother lay dying in her house. She died at home because Mom refused to send her to a nursing home.

I thought that was very sweet, but I never told her that, either.

I think we both know, my mother and I, that tomorrow is not promised. Her health could fail her and I could get killed on some Southern California freeway. I think about this a lot.

It's further evidence that we need to work through our guilt and realize that we are just two imperfect people in an imperfect world.

I'd like to hear from her.

I'd like to hear that even though I've stumbled along the way, I've achieved most of what I said I would. Done what I wanted to. Won awards. Have permanent hand prints on my back from it being patted so often. Earned the respect and admiration of my colleagues.

But I've never once heard my mom say she was proud of me.

I'd like to hear that she is.

I'd like to hear that instead of how much she likes my flat or my outfit—one that she has inevitably bought. I'd like to hear how it was living through the Great Depression, two world wars, my breach birth. I'd like to know how she survived the turbulent sixties. What it was like to have a hysterectomy, survive cancer, and own more than one hundred pairs of bluejeans.

I'd like to hear how it feels to have put two kids through college. How it feels to be a grandmother. And if she still has those dreams of me walking down the aisle.

Mostly, I would like to know how difficult it's been to love a kid like me. One who can't tell her how much she means to me. Or that everything I am, every ounce of success I've enjoyed, is because of her.

Maybe someday soon we will *talk*.

2

About
Black Men

Dwight Lewis

THE TENNESSEAN

Where Are the Fathers?

was almost through with my visit to Nashville's Caldwell Early Childhood Learning Center when the principal looked me straight in the eye and asked: "Mr. Lewis, where are the black fathers?"

Being a father of a sixteen-year-old son, I was somewhat puzzled by the question as Myron Oglesby-Pitts asked again: "Where are the black fathers? Ninety percent of the 250 students here at Caldwell are black, and of that number, only six fathers have shown up this school year to see about their children.

"Where are the black fathers? When my school doors open, I see moms come up but hardly ever any fathers. Where are they?"

By the sincere look on her face, you could tell that Pitts was very concerned. Then she said, "I want the black fathers to come forth. You have to do more than just bring a baby into this world to be a real father. And if the biological fathers don't come forward, I'm calling on other strong African-American men to come and fill their shoes."

She added, "When I see the few fathers come here I get overwhelmed. I need them to help out with the children. I have volunteers who come here to help, but I want to see the natural fathers marching forward.

"When I have a father come forth, you can see the difference in how a child acts. Some of them seem to have a little more respect for adulthood when a man is present."

As Pitts—a middle-aged black woman—paused for a moment, another voice said, "I will tell you where the black fathers are. Most of them are in jail or they've run off and left their kids behind."

The voice was that of John Scott, one of the few black male figures that Pitts sees from time to time at her east Nashville school. The Caldwell Early Childhood Learning Center is located next to a public housing development that is plagued by violence, drugs, and poverty.

"You don't see a lot of fathers out here," said Scott, fifty-seven, who has a nephew at Caldwell. "Most of the time you see their brothers or some other relative.

"If Martin Luther King were alive today, he would have a heart attack over what's taking place with our black fathers."

As I left Caldwell, I couldn't forget the question Pitts asked— "Where are the black fathers?"

Nor could I forget the answer given by John Scott.

I'm a black father and I'm not in jail, I thought to myself. I also have several friends who are good fathers and they aren't in jail.

Maybe Pitts and Scott just haven't seen the black fathers that I know. There are some around and they're being good parents.

But then I remembered something I had read in the National Urban League's State of Black America 1994 report.

It said: "While the vast majority of the 10 million African-American households are family households (that is, the household members are related by birth, marriage, or adoption), only about half the families were headed by a married couple in 1990, down from 68% in 1970 and 56% in 1980."

The report added: "These trends profoundly affect all members of the urban African-American community: men, women, youth, the elderly and most dramatically, children. The proportion of African-American children living with two parents declined from 58% in 1970 to 38% in 1990. By the year 2000, the proportion of African-American children living with both parents will decline to 24%."

Then there was the *USA Today* story a few years ago that said. "The incarceration rate for black males in the USA is four times South Africa's—3,109 per 100,000 in the USA, compared with 729 in South Africa."

Those are scary statistics. Suddenly, I found myself asking the question: "Where are the black fathers?"

Then NAACP Executive Director Ben Chavis, who was in Nashville that day attending the eighth annual convention of the 100 Black Men of America Inc., said, "Obviously, the 100 Black Men are doing a good job of being paternal fathers to the children they visit in schools around the United States. Overall, I think black fathers get a bum rap. I'm not saying there aren't any problems, but the majority of black fathers are struggling, working, and making an impact in the community in which they live, and they are helping to raise their children."

What he said prompted responses from others attending the 100 Black Men convention at Nashville's Opryland Hotel.

"If you were to tour the inner city, you would find many black fathers standing on street corners," said Dr. Herman Reese of Atlanta, vice president for programs for the organization. "They are unemployed and then there are a disproportionate number of black fathers in prison. Our challenge is to get these fathers off the streets and out of prison into something meaningful for us and them. We've got to start some type of domestic urban core program to help these men.

"If you look at the statistics, you will see that there are too many babies being born to unwed mothers. We've got to make our black men sensitive to the fact that these are their children and they can't just drop babies and not take care of them, or interact with them."

Then there was Andrew Young, the former congressman from Georgia and U.S. ambassador, who said, "Black fathers are working two jobs to take care of their families. I resent people defining African-American males by saying all of them are pimps, drug pushers, and rap artists. Every time I go to church, I'm amazed at the number of young men I see there. Yes, we have problems, but the majority of black fathers are working hard to make ends meet."

Young, the author of *A Way Out of No Way: The Spiritual Memoirs of Andrew Young*, added, "There are a lot of insecurities in the black male these days because they feel threatened by whites and they don't feel they're getting the support they need from black women, like their moms gave their dads."

So where are the black fathers?

My answer to Pitts, the Caldwell principal, is that indeed there are too many black fathers in prison.

The result being that many of our children are running the streets unsupervised and in many instances following in their fathers' footsteps.

And there are too many black fathers standing on street corners, not caring what happens to their children when they are in school.

We need to be there with the teachers to lend a helping hand and to encourage our children to get a good education so they can have a better life than we've had.

Like Herman Reese said, we've got to come up with programs to encourage our men and children to be good fathers. Those of us who are doing pretty good in life must communicate with those who have had it rough. We must let them know that we'll do what we can to help them find a better way.

But the majority of black fathers, like Ben Chavis and Andy Young said, are there with their families. Many are indeed struggling to make ends meet. And often it's difficult, but they don't give up.

I think about my father, who died of cancer in 1990; I was forty-two when he died at age sixty-five. Never did I hear him say, "I don't care about my children."

He did say once while he was sick that there were times when he got tired while working, but he never stopped.

My father was not rich, monetarily, but he always saw to it that there was food on our table and clothes on our backs. He also worked hard to make sure that his children received a good education. And he taught us that religion should be an important part of our lives.

Most black fathers are willing to struggle like my father did.

"I've done it," said Walter Hunt, head of the Metro Action Commission, in Nashville. "I'm fifty-five, and my son is sixteen. His mother and I divorced when our son was eighteen months old, and I've had him ever since. It's been tough sometimes, but I've tried to be there for him to make sure he's had sound direction and good parameters.

"There have been times when I traveled because of other jobs I've had, and often I would take my son with me. It hasn't been easy, but he's worth it."

Sure, all black fathers aren't with their families or with their children.

But most of us are. And those of us who are doing well—black men and women in this case—should reach out to those black fathers who aren't doing so well so we can bring them along.

If not, it won't be long before a lot more of us are asking the question: Where are the black fathers?

Harold Jackson

BALTIMORE SUN

A Message to Black Men

Pieces of dog were strewn across the highway. Some poor, dumb animal had exploded upon impact with a speeding vehicle. By the look of things, it probably was hit by one of those huge 18-wheelers.

I kept driving, thinking about the dead animal, then about human lives taken prematurely: Martin Luther King, Jr., Otis Redding, Arthur Ashe. My eyes stayed tuned to the road as my mind drifted in the opposite direction, to lives that seem inexhaustible. I thought of 101-year-old A. G. Gaston.

Not just since I was a child, but since my mother was a child, Arthur George Gaston's life has provided a Horatio Alger story for black Americans. His rags-to-riches success has been the encouragement countless parents, teachers, and ministers have used to push black children to strive harder.

When I was growing up, the story of this black multimillionaire was inspirational even to the most economically deprived residents of the housing project where I lived.

But to many of today's young African-Americans, living in seemingly unconquerable poverty, A. G. Gaston's story is just another fairy tale. They cannot make the connection between his economic struggle and their desperately poor lives.

The percentage of African-Americans living poor has not significantly changed since President Lyndon B. Johnson declared war on poverty in 1965. It's still more than 30 percent. Almost half of all black children live in a family considered poor by federal government standards.

The black unemployment rate, at nearly 14 percent, continues to hover at about double the rate for whites. Unemployment among black teenagers is chronic, nearly 40 percent. The median family income for blacks is about $15,000 a year less than it is for white families.

Only about 11 percent of blacks get a college education, compared to 20 percent of whites. The life expectancy of a black person is four years less than a white's. A fourth of all black men ages 20 to 29 are either in jail, in prison, or under a parole officer's supervision. And the beat goes on.

Those harsh realities, coupled with the prevailing attitude of the Ronald Reagan eighties, that poor people have only themselves to blame for their condition, has stifled the hopes of many young black Americans. The Clinton Administration offers promise, but has not restored that hope.

Without hope, young people think little of the future. They live for today, taking chances that anyone who thought he had a future would never take. They sell dope, smoke crack, pack guns, practice promiscuity, shun education, and spurn religion. A. G. Gaston? He can't tell them a thing.

These young people believe whatever Gaston suffered while fighting the prejudice of a Jim Crow system to become a financial success was nothing compared to the dangers of living "in the 'hood" today. You judge.

Gaston was born in a log cabin in rural Marengo County, Alabama, less than forty years after American slavery ended. He grew up during a period of this nation's history when lynching black people was about as common as shooting off fireworks on the Fourth of July.

During his early childhood, Gaston and his mother lived with his grandparents, who had been slaves. Gaston's mother later became the cook for a wealthy white family in Birmingham and they moved there, but the privileges this new urban lifestyle afforded Gaston were few.

Mrs. Gaston enrolled her son in the Carrie A. Tuggle Institute for Colored Children. "Granny" Tuggle, the daughter of a Mohawk Indian chief and a black woman, was also a former slave. She was totally committed to the education of black children, and Gaston, to this day, credits her with teaching him how to treat people as you would like to be treated.

It was at Tuggle School that Gaston learned about the man who became his personal inspiration, Booker T. Washington. Washington, a champion of black capitalism and the founder of what is now called Tuskegee University, made a speech at Tuggle that Gaston never forgot.

Washington said opportunity is like a bald-headed man with only a patch of hair right in front. You have to grab that tuft of hair, grasp the opportunity while it's confronting you, or else you'll be grasping at a slick bald head.

That tuft of hair was more like a few sparse strands for a young black man in early-twentieth-century America. Gaston decided to try his luck in the Army. He had already been in the service three years by the time this country entered World War I. He served with distinction as part of an all-black unit in France, the 317th Ammunition train of the 92nd Rainbow Division.

Like the next world war, the First World War greatly raised the expectations of black soldiers. Their near-equal treatment as members of the U.S. armed forces in countries that did not have as strict a racial caste system made them believe they really would be coming home as "conquering heroes."

But in his 1968 book, *Green Power*, Gaston talks about the Army's efforts to nip in the bud any uppity thoughts the black troops might be getting at World War I's end. The Army had Tuskegee Institute's administrator, Dr. Robert R. Moton, speak to the black soldiers prior to their disembarking.

"The Negroes were looking for it to be equal rights back then. We were all prepared for it," Gaston said. "It was a cold spirit when Dr. Moton came and advised us to stay in our place. But I was a follower of Booker T. Washington, and I followed his advice. I always stayed in my place."

Gaston came back to Birmingham and got a job as a laborer at Tennessee Coal and Iron Company that paid $3.10 a day. But Gaston was still looking for his bald-headed man. The other workers at the plant so liked the portions of his home-prepared lunch he would share with them that it gave him an idea.

He began selling box lunches prepared by his mother. And with the additional capital, he made loans to co-workers who needed money for dates. Borrowers had to pay him 25 cents on the dollar, every two weeks. Somehow, Gaston also found spare time to operate a popcorn and peanuts stand.

During this period of entrepreneurial frenzy, Gaston came upon the idea that would change his life forever. He noticed that even the stingiest of the steel plant workers would chip in whenever preachers came around begging for donations to bury a black pauper.

Gaston decided to start a burial society for the black workers at TCI. He got a lot of verbal encouragement from his co-workers, but few backed up their words with cash. Consequently, when the first member of the society died there was only $30 in the pot to pay for a $100 funeral.

Gaston was able to get the woman buried on credit, but the burial society idea appeared ready for a eulogy itself. It was saved when a local minister, the Rev. S. H. Ravizee of Hopewell Baptist Church, told his flock he wasn't going to beg money for funerals anymore. He suggested they join Gaston's burial society instead.

That was around 1923. It wasn't long after that that Gaston had enough money to buy a mortuary and open Smith and Gaston Funeral Directors. In 1932, the burial society was incorporated as Booker T. Washington Insurance Co., the launching pad for all his other successes.

In 1939, Gaston started Booker T. Washington Business College to train black clerical workers. In 1947, he acquired New Grace Hill Cemetery. In 1954, he opened the Gaston Motel in downtown Birmingham because black travelers didn't have a place to stay in the city. In 1957, he and a group of investors began Citizens Federal Savings and Loan, which is now a full service bank.

The investors raised $350,000 to start the bank; today it has assets exceeding $70 million. Booker T. Washington Insurance Co., which Gaston sold to an employee stock ownership program in 1987, has assets approaching $40 million. The Gaston empire also includes a construction company, a home for senior citizens, a real estate company, a drugstore, and an AM-FM radio station.

Success wasn't handed to Gaston on a platter. He grew up poor. He didn't have to guess whether he was discriminated against because he was an African-American. The threat that jealous whites might strike out at such a prosperous black man was constant.

Gaston was told to stay in his place, and he did, for the most part. But he still managed to do more than just survive. He succeeded where other businessmen, black or white, failed. Listening to his story reveals how.

Gaston's health has been poor since he suffered a stroke in January 1992. He shuns interviews. But four weeks after his release from the hospital he was back at his desk at Citizens Federal. Not long after that I had a chance to sit down and talk with him about his life.

His speech was halting, at times slurred, but his mind was razor sharp. He remembered being called an Uncle Tom in the 1960s, for although he helped civil rights leaders behind the scenes he was never visible at demonstrations.

"I was always a good nigger," Gaston said. "But there was a reason for that. It allowed me to take advantage of opportunity."

Because he was a millionaire, Gaston was often invited to meetings of Birmingham's most influential businessmen.

"I was the only nigger in the group, you know, and had money, too," he said. "I got opportunity because of that. I got the franchise for the radio station. I never would have gotten it if I hadn't been a good nigger. I took advantage of my position, of being smart with white people."

Being smart with white people. It's a concept that goes back at least to the beginning of that so-called peculiar institution,

American slavery, itself. Black people survived slavery not because they were the physically superior beasts that whites wanted them to be. Black people survived slavery because they used their intellect.

They learned well the lesson of the flexible rod; it does not break like the rigid one. Certainly there were many acts of defiance, acts of rebellion against slavery. But there were also many acts of cunning, whereby blacks put up a front of acquiescence while working behind that facade for freedom. Slavery's end may have elevated this tactic to an art form, especially in the Jim Crow South, where African-Americans feigned ingratiating respect for the white folks they worked for by day and cursed at night.

It was no coincidence that the civil rights movement reached its heights in the South. Blacks in Dixie were no more the accepting darkies that actor Stepin Fetchit played than he was when he wiped off his makeup. But they knew how to bend and how to straighten up, when it was time.

Gaston, the "good nigger," stood tall when the burial society he created was almost taken from him in its infancy by a white man who coveted the profitable venture.

When the owner of the funeral home Gaston bought died while Gaston was still paying off the mortgage, the man's son claimed he had not only inherited the funeral home from his father but also the Booker T. Washington Burial Society.

The claim was ludicrous, but it was a white man's word against a black's in the Jim Crow South. Gaston sought help from a white lawyer popular in the black community who advised the scheming heir that "the best thing you can do is leave that nigger alone and get out of the whole thing."

The heir refused to give up and had the police chief of Fairfield attempt to seize the burial society's records. Gaston had given the documents to another African-American of the South who knew when to stand up to white folks. After "Mother" Lewis, the wife of one of Gaston's funeral home employees, finished tongue-lashing the chief, he scurried home.

The heir eventually gave up, but other whites jealous of a black man's success harassed Gaston. He said his funeral car drivers were constantly getting traffic tickets, even when they parked in front of the funeral home. He didn't give up, although he did finally move from the Fairfield suburb into Birmingham.

The bend-but-don't-break philosophy was apparent in 1957 when Gaston came to the aid of blacks in Tuskegee who were conducting an economic boycott of white-owned stores to gain their voting rights. The white banks were putting pressure on all those participating in the boycott who had outstanding mortgages or loans. Gaston promised to advance mortgage money to anyone who needed it.

When the civil rights struggle reached a crescendo in Birmingham in 1963, Gaston provided lodging for Martin Luther King, Jr., the Rev. Ralph Abernathy, and other movement leaders from out of town. Racists knew what Gaston was doing; his motel was bombed as a result. Gaston also provided bail money for demonstrators on many occasions.

He was no Uncle Tom, he just knew when to bend without breaking, how to play the role of "good nigger" until playacting would no longer do. There was nothing unusual about Gaston's methodology. It was the way black children were brought up from the end of the Civil War into the civil rights era.

I grew up in a segregated society in the 1950s and 1960s. My interaction with whites was minimal until I reached my senior year of high school. The year my school closed, and I was forced to attend one that as a result of new desegregation laws became mixed, 50-50, almost overnight.

As a child, however, even though I was rarely around whites, I learned through the actions and remarks of my parents and other adults, that black people were expected to tolerate behavior from white people that they would not from their own, expected to bend but not break.

It wasn't that black children were taught that white people were superior. They were taught that white people were untrustworthy and thus had to be treated carefully. If you didn't respect the white person, you feigned respect until you could get out of his presence because you couldn't trust him to treat you as an equal if you addressed him as one.

I will never forget the first lesson in racism I received, the one that taught me to be always on my guard when encountering whites. I think I was nine, which means King had not yet come to Birmingham to integrate public accommodations, but the movement, led by the Rev. Fred Shuttlesworth, was making progress.

It was not unusual for me to walk to the grocery store ten blocks away for my mother or a neighbor. The only major thoroughfare to be crossed was Sixth Avenue South, which emptied onto Lomb Avenue where Elmwood Cemetery was located. Elmwood is in a black neighborhood, but at the time blacks could not be buried there.

Like most nine-year-olds, I walked with my head down, always looking for some discarded item that could be added to my collection of treasure—a distinctive bottle cap, perhaps a coin, maybe an irregularly shaped rock or shiny pebble.

I purchased whatever it was I was sent to the store for and began the walk back home. I waited at the intersection of Sixth Avenue and Goldwire Street, two blocks from the cemetery, for the traffic light to change. It did. Perhaps I took a quick glance at the ground to make sure I hadn't missed any potential booty.

Just as I was about to step into the street I looked up into the face of an oncoming pickup truck and stepped back, barely missing having my foot taken off by the speeding vehicle. And then I heard it: "Nigger! Nigger!"

In the back of the pickup were three stringy-haired, dirty-blond, skinny white boys in overalls, sans shirts, all about my age, grinning and screaming the racial epithet at me. I never saw the truck driver, but have always imagined him as some uneducated spawn of an uneducated spawn who was making sure his children followed in his bigoted footsteps.

I was horrified, and not just because my brief life had almost ended. I was shocked by the verbal venom hurled at me by people who didn't even know me. I didn't hate white people. In my strictly segregated world I was never around whites and consequently never considered their racism.

Still shaking as I walked home, I wondered what would make them hate black people so much they would risk killing a black child. Weren't they afraid of the consequences? Obviously not.

The goal in those days was to avoid confrontation with white people because nine times out of ten, if not more, the white person was going to win in the end. The deck was stacked in his favor. Only after the civil rights movement brought more equal treatment in the courts and at the ballot box did this attitude change.

But the change was dramatic. The black power component of the struggle sought not only to gain equal rights but to compensate for African-Americans' lack of self-esteem and past willingness to bend to the whims of whites until there was no more room to bend.

Martin King taught black children to stand up for their God-given rights and challenge authority when it is wrong. The Black Panthers taught black children to take what should be theirs and disregard white authority because it is illegitimate.

The legacy of the Panthers' ideology remains prevalent in urban black communities today, ironically, even as former Panthers, in their daily dealings with white folks today, have become as flexible as Martin King ever was.

When activist Angela Davis was on the run in the 1970s, she didn't have to fear capture by the FBI while hiding out in Birmingham, her hometown. Panther ideology, which said you never turn a black person in to the police, was pervasive in Birmingham's black community as well as in other urban black communities throughout the nation.

That ideology said the white man was the enemy. Since all authority in this nation was derivative of the white man, authority had no legitimacy in the black community. The tool of authority, the police, was also the enemy, the object of derision, not respect. Incidents of police brutality during the civil rights era and beyond helped to ingrain that attitude toward the police.

Now, decades after the Panthers' demise, their rejection-of-authority, don't-cooperate-with-the-police, never-bend philosophy can still be seen in urban areas where young African-Americans take the cool pose of "gangsta" rappers, rejecting all authority and anything else they can label "white."

The strokes of their brush are, of course, too broad. Black

children who want to escape poverty by pursuing an education that requires they learn how to speak and write grammatically correct are accused of acting "white," a treasonous offense.

This rejection of all authority, especially that of the "enemy" police, has helped make black neighborhoods the haven of drug dealers and other criminals who know they can count on the "brothers and sisters" adhering to the same code of silence that benefited political fugitives such as Angela Davis.

Sure, many black people refuse to cooperate with the police out of fear of retribution by the criminals. But also prevalent is a twisted belief among many others that to tell the police anything is itself a crime.

They cannot forget that Birmingham's Bull Connor–led police force in 1963 tried to beat black people into submission. They keep seeing the Los Angeles and Detroit police forces of today, which obviously still believe Connor was on the right track when he urged officers to whip first, ask questions later.

A consequence of the reject-authority attitude is that almost any black person on the opposite side of the law is seen as either a victim or a hero. Even the wrongdoers such as the black men arrested for viciously attacking a white truck driver after the Rodney King trial verdict were considered by many blacks as political prisoners rather than thugs.

This attitude that all authority is corrupt, which goes beyond the typical rejection of authority figures exhibited by youngsters of any hue in modern America, is particularly harmful to young African-American males when attached to the accompanying rejection of their parents' bend-but-don't-break philosophy.

Attempting to prove their individuality, many are actually leading cookie-cutter lives that call for them to eat, drink, dress, speak, and sleep the same way—what they perceive to be the nonwhite way.

Ironically, many young whites seeking a rebellious identity are emulating the same speech and dress. (I practically stopped wearing my "X" baseball cap after the Macy's department stores started selling Spike Lee merchandise using white models to wear the garments in their advertising.)

Young black men, trying hard to fit a mold that is more confining than they realize, fail to see the danger within the limits of the stereotype they have created for themselves, a stereotype that is in many ways more damaging than anything Amos and Andy ever did or said.

These young men fail to see how easy they make it for the "enemy" to justify putting the same label on all young African-American males. A crime is committed, pick up any one of them, they're all the same, aren't they? Just one more "gangsta" off the streets.

Much has been written in recent years about the imminent extinction of the African-American male. There is certainly evidence of his demise, what with so many dying early, violent deaths, others languishing in prison, and too many more addicted to drugs to make their existence meaningful.

If black men are to prove the doomsayers wrong, they must take a lesson from the Earth's prehistory. They should look at the creatures that were once the most powerful on earth, the dinosaurs, who no longer exist because they refused to adapt. The dinosaurs wouldn't bend, consequently they broke.

There are countless other creatures walking the face of this world, swimming in its oceans or streams, or burrowing beneath its dirt that existed in some form when dinosaurs ruled. Unlike the dinosaurs, however, they changed when change was necessary to ensure survival.

We know mankind is capable of change. His adaptability has allowed him to live through all the fits and throes a changing Earth could toss. The black man has shown his ability to adapt to the most trying of situations, slavery among them, and bend as much as necessary to live through it and go on.

The black man's current plight must be treated the same way. He must see that strength lies in his ability to look at a situation, determine what change in strategy is necessary to conquer it, and proceed accordingly.

Young black men must be strong, strong enough to believe they can change, they can bend, because if they don't they will perish.

Young black men must see they will continue to be vulnerable to joblessness unless they get a good education. They must stop dismissing those who want to be educated as wanting to be white. They must respect the young brothers and sisters who make good grades as they do the ones who are good athletes.

We must never forget our own heritage and work hard to have the contributions of our ancestors included in American and world history textbooks. But black students need not fear learning from a Eurocentric perspective.

The American education system was created by people of European descent. Those are the cards we have been dealt, but we have shown by our achievements that we can win with them. Some of this country's greatest thinkers, educators, inventors, physicians, writers, etc., have been African-American products of this nation's public schools.

One wonders whether those of European ancestry, if forcefully placed in a world so different culturally from that of their ancestors, would be able to achieve intellectually what the black man has in the United States since slavery.

Young black men must also see they will continue to be vulnerable to disease until they live healthier lives. That means giving up the drug culture that kills both the dispensers and partakers of illegal substances. It means accepting the fact that wanton promiscuity in a world with AIDS is like kissing death on the mouth.

They must see that extinction is the future of any species that takes the opposite gender for granted, calling its members by derogatory names that suggest they are worthless except for use as another means to fleeting gratification.

The world is changing. The very term "working class" is taking on a brand-new meaning as technology is rapidly taking us to the day when there simply won't be enough jobs to go around. The number of people who are no longer counted in unemployment statistics because they have given up on looking for work keep growing.

Too many young black men are among that group. They will remain among the exploitable ranks of the nonworking, dependent either on the welfare state or criminal activity for their livelihood, so long as they are unwilling to bend, unwilling to learn.

Of course, flexibility alone is not enough. A. G. Gaston certainly learned you can bend over backwards and some white people will still keep pushing until you fall. You have to know when to stand up and push back. You have to let people know your willingness to compromise is a sign of strength, not weakness.

Perhaps it was easier for Gaston to bend when he was a young man. Even with Jim Crow at its peak, there was the promise of better days for black people in America.

In the aftermath of the civil rights era, it's easy to lose sight of hope with so many economic and social barriers erected by whites still facing African-Americans, with so many whites unwilling to accept the fact that the debt to black people who endured slavery and second-class citizenship has not been paid.

But hope remains. Black people, particularly young African-American men, must realize they do not have to live the lives of despair some whites want to reserve for them. They do not have to accept a world of poverty and disease and hopelessness.

They must have the strength, the courage, the desire to adapt to this changing world, bending and flexing and—by any means necessary—making the moves it takes to progress, to go forward, to reach the day when racism cannot exist because skin color is no longer a condition of power.

It's OK to bend; if you don't, you might break.

Howard Bryant

OAKLAND TRIBUNE

The Search for Role Models

A while back, I was assigned to venture into the inner city to look for role models, to find those pillars of strength who keep city kids from entering crack houses.

This was designed to be a wonderfully triumphant human interest piece. Instead, it amounted to another in a string of naive but slightly well-meaning assignments designed to find hope in a black community where white people saw none.

There is also a footnote to this tale. The originator of the story idea figured it was best to pass it on, because, in his words, he didn't "feel quite comfortable leaving his car unattended in Oakland and walking around unsupervised." He was white. I wasn't surprised.

A nefarious undercurrent was at work. This assignment was circumscribed only to the "inner city." Read that "black people." If there was an economic issue at work, surely low-income white kids also needed someone to look up to. So why just inner city?

I was cynical. Role models aren't something that exist for the general populace. A person has to be chosen by another to be a role model, regardless of credentials. One person's role model could be—and usually is—another person's nightmare.

But being the low person on the totem pole, and serious about a long career in the news business, I was a good little soldier and carried out the assignment.

On nearly every corner along San Pablo Avenue in West Oakland was a reminder of ugly neglect. A liquor store adjacent to a church; between 20th and 33rd Streets, prostitutes held court.

Meanwhile, kids walked home from school, bright-colored backpacks slung around both shoulders, happy-faced and oblivious. As in neighborhoods with white picket fences, some parents met their kids at the corner. Other children walked home alone, aloof to the boarded-up storefronts and vacant lots.

I caught up with Jermaine Hill for lunch. Hill and his mother run the Eastwood Group Home in East Oakland, designed for kids whose home lives for one reason or other became a disaster. We were talking about Darrnaryl Stamps, a promising nineteen-year-old basketball player who had recently opted to attend junior college instead of a Division I basketball school.

If the newspapers are the primary source of information for most people, Stamps was rendered a virtual derelict—or merely another black male—by the press. He had talent to block rebounds and dunk basketballs, but after three unsuccessful attempts at the Scholastic Aptitude Test, Stamps was a failure. The papers said that due to "failing to achieve a minimum score of 700 on his SAT," Darrnaryl Stamps would not be attending San Jose State. From that point on, Stamps didn't exist. End of story.

But Stamps was more than a student at McClymonds High School in West Oakland. In the framework of keeping his black family together, Stamps, from age fifteen, was his family's boat, anchor, and life preserver.

Stamps dropped out of McClymonds High School nearly before he got started, quitting altogether in the ninth grade. After returning, he spent the next three years at different addresses. At a lanky 6′ 8″ and 215 pounds, he lived in his mother's house, sleeping on a couch nearly half his size. He lived at his grandmother's house for a time, and then with a friend before finally landing at Eastwood.

It was with Hill that Stamps turned things around. Darrnaryl posted a 3.0 grade point average in his final year, while being named class president.

Hill deflected praise. "It wasn't me. It was Darrnaryl. He had to want to do this. I couldn't go to class for him. He had to want it. He wanted a better environment."

In his senior year, Stamps provided $1,300 for his family. That's pretty impressive for a high school kid who is juggling the hats of class president, star basketball player, and solid-B student. But it was more. Stamps's $1,300 was the *only* money generated for his family. His mother's tax statement revealed she did not work for the entire year. His sister, only thirteen, was too young to work.

Thirteen hundred dollars was expected to feed, house, and clothe three people. Stamps, meanwhile, gained all-city honors as Oakland's best power forward. Thirteen hundred dollars determined the lives of three people.

If nothing else, to say Stamps or any other black person needed someone to look up to in order to avoid the pitfalls of inner-city life is a joke. It is not unlike throwing up one's hands and accepting the status quo.

Instead of a "positive role model," all Darrnaryl Stamps really could have used was a few more dollars.

When dealing with many white people about the fate and future of black people, I would expect nothing less than an easy, shortsighted assessment. But in considering an apparent void of leadership for black people, it is wise to first consider that black America, and especially its children, are dealing with a much greater and terrifying force.

According to the *Wall Street Journal*, African-American workers were the only racial group to experience a net loss of jobs in the recession of 1990–1991. Black employment fell in six of nine major industry groups.

At the Dial Corporation, African-American workers lost 43.6 percent of all jobs cut, though blacks made up only 26.3 percent of the company's workforce.

The Equal Employment Opportunity Commission found that nearly a third of all blue-collar jobs lost during that time belonged to African-Americans.

Conversely, 53,548 jobs were created by the service industry, but black people lost 16,630 jobs in the service sector during that period of "growth."

The point is this: whatever leadership void that exists in the black community cannot compare to historical barriers that have been erected to destroy that community.

Simply put, if all the role models in the world descended on the city of Oakland, little would change as long as these barriers remain.

In 1992, Citibank rejected 67 percent of all black applicants for housing loans, while the refusal rates for whites was 41 percent. During that same time, Bank of America approved only 3 percent of African-American loan applications, while approving 71 percent of loan requests from whites.

In Milwaukee, only 30 percent of black applicants received loans, against a 79.8 approval rating for whites. In many cases, the black people who were rejected earned a higher annual income than whites who were approved for loans of equal or greater amounts.

The dilapidated homes, vacant lots, and boarded-up storefronts in West Oakland, surrounded by good, hardworking black people, slowly seemed to make a little more sense.

More than anything else, the systematic desertion of the black community as a political priority coupled with a tumultuous home life set Darrnaryl Stamps on precarious footing. But as an individual, Stamps was no closer to a crack house than a white kid learning Shakespeare at an East Coast prep school.

This is the umbrella under which African-Americans reside. The hypocrisy would be funny, if not for its hurtful consequences. For each image and societal malady that afflicts black people, the solution is not to examine the various components (like redlining black neighborhoods) that may contribute to the current peril. Instead, it is thought there is a lack of role models and the remedy is simply to find more. It is this all-encompassing but amorphous creature—the black role model—who is called upon to stop our bleeding.

Where is Stamps now? He's attending college in Utah. He's

playing basketball, studying for difficult classes, and enjoying campus life as would any other college freshman, black or white.

It occurs to me that if Darrnaryl Stamps did need a role model or hero to help him through the turbulent times, he didn't have to look any further than a mirror because there wasn't a person on earth with a big, fat sneakers-endorsement contract that could have done a better job than he's done for himself.

Claude Lewis

PHILADELPHIA INQUIRER

Memories of
James Baldwin

**He taught me many
fundamental lessons
about writing and
about life.**

The late James Baldwin was twelve years older than I—and one hundred years wiser. He encouraged me to write, not for newspapers, but for myself.

"You can't be YOU in somebody else's newspaper," he warned. And in a way, I suppose he was right.

But I came along at a time when people sought safety; I wanted a job and what I thought was the protection of a regular paycheck. I had a child, Pamela, the first of four children.

Baldwin's family was his mother, brothers and sisters, some cousins, nieces and nephews. He had responsibilities, but viewed them as those he inherited, not those he created.

He charged, politely, that I was using my family as an excuse not to jump cleanly into the water, preferring to wade "near the safety of the journalistic shoreline." I disagreed, but deep down inside I wasn't so sure he was wrong. Though he's been dead for years now, his words continue to haunt me.

Baldwin understood that it was required of any serious writer to experience and suffer the awful risks inherent in earning their living from the written word. Those risks "come with the territory," was his way of putting it.

Thirty years ago, he seemed too aggressive to me, too bitter, too inflexible, and too unforgiving. Back then, I was convinced progress would arrive over time. He was offended by that and told me so. He taught me—and I shall never forget the lesson—that time can be both constructive or destructive, that freedom "seldom rolls in on the wheels of inevitability." He paused, the way only Baldwin could pause, to let his major point sink in, then flashed his enigmatic smile.

We spent many hours in Harlem, along with his brother David, drinking what I now realize was much too much, discussing whether white people would ever fully embrace blacks (it was Negroes in those days), and whether blacks would ever be allowed into mainstream America.

We'd visit several of Harlem's famous night spots of the period. Most often, it was either Sugar Ray Robinson's place, once located between 122nd and 123rd Streets and Seventh Avenue, or Small's Paradise, on the corner of 135th Street and Seventh Avenue, or Well's Chicken and Waffle Restaurant, which reopened at 2247 Adam Clayton Powell Boulevard.

Strangers who admired his writing stopped to shake his hand. Baldwin was unfailingly courteous and friendly, but quickly returned to our exchanges at the bar. Sometimes our conversations became pretty intense. On occasion, other patrons at the bar would stand close, listening to arguments from both sides. Invariably, Jimmy would "win."

I never minded not winning for, after all, I was there to learn; Jimmy was there to exercise his keen mind. Most often, he would offer far more compelling arguments than his adversaries. Just the fact that he thought enough of me to spend his time with me was a pretty fair exchange, considering what he had accomplished and what he had to share.

One of the things that often bothered him was how much time people wasted discussing what white people think about the issue of race. ("We know what they think. We see it in the way they live, in their literary productions, and the way they perceive others," he argued.)

During one of those conversations, Baldwin startled me, as he often could: "Do you suppose, when they are alone, that white people spend such an inordinate amount of time arguing about Negroes as we spend arguing about white people?"

The Baldwins were bright men, not because of what they'd learned in schools, but because of what they'd learned in life. However, racial discrimination seemed to have kept them in a constant state of rage.

I remember asking Jimmy why he left America. Why he went to Europe, which was even more white than America.

"No, it isn't more white than America," he scolded. "That would be impossible! Most Europeans have white skin, but they are not captured by it; they do not worship it in the way that white Americans do, you see.

"Now, to get to your other point. You make it sound so, uh, casual. I didn't *leave* this land, I *fled* it in order to survive. If I had remained, I would have gone to jail, become a junkie, or I would have wound up in an insane asylum."

Several people, standing by and listening, burst into applause when Baldwin closed his mouth. They applauded his precision of words and his understanding of his nation.

Inevitably, we went our separate ways. He to Europe, I to a job with *Newsweek* magazine. When next we met—I think it may have been four years later—we did the perfunctory thing. We hugged, smiled, he asked how I had been, and then, with an orchestrated innocence, he posed, "What are you doing these days?"

I didn't want to answer. Jimmy and I knew what was coming. I had not taken his advice and could not tell him that I was working on some great novel or series of essays or plays. I was at *Newsweek* and not feeling very good about it. *Newsweek* was group journalism in those days and I was not proud of my role.

Back then, one would write a story and by the time it made its way down the line of editors, one could hardly recognize his original work. But it was a job, and among those who didn't know better, *Newsweek* was a prestigious place to work.

I was about to read and review his *The Fire Next Time*, the book of essays that catapulted Baldwin into star status among the literary set.

I was both astounded and shaken by the book. Not so much

by what he wrote, but by its beautiful simplicity and its frightening power. His essays were the most forceful, clear, efficient, direct, angry, exploratory, accusatory, and logical essays I had ever read.

They affected me greatly and I knew, immediately, that he was an unusually gifted and authentic writer and thinker, a permanent performer that America had produced despite our nation's poisonous attitude toward blacks.

James Baldwin, with his massive gifts, his controlled anger, his blunt way of saying what was on his mind, turned out to be a joke on racism. There was nothing inferior about him. He was all strength, all intelligence, all intuition when it came to the issue of race in America.

He was a dark little man with moist and protruding eyes and the most beautiful and expressive mind I had encountered. What made Baldwin so powerful was that he had discovered a certain truth, found it in the fear and vulnerability he grew up with in the world's most famous ghetto—Harlem—where his father forced him to be a child evangelist for three years.

In spite of his anger, he never gave up hope that black and white America would ultimately unite. But Baldwin was bitter, and had every right to be, because with all his talent and energy and insight, his country would not give him the recognition he deserved—no, EARNED.

I honestly believe that Baldwin tried to hate his homeland. It was one of the few efforts at which he failed. When major events occurred in black America, no matter where he was in the world he had to arrive at home to be at the center of them.

Though he loved France, because that nation appreciated and acknowledged his great gifts, he never became a Frenchman. He was an American and, in spite of his irrevocable hostility toward his nation, his loyalties were to his country and its people—all of them, the black and the white.

That is why he arranged to be returned home from St. Paul de Vence, France, for burial. There was no way he could rest in peace so far from the scene of so many of the most heinous racial crimes in all of human history.

Throughout his existence, Baldwin's huge eyes mirrored his troubled soul. With eyes such as his, there was no way he could hide the hurt and anger. It was etched into his existence, like words carved in stone.

The last time I saw him was in September 1986. I had played a small role in bringing his play, *Amen Corner*, to the Philadelphia Drama/Annenberg Center Theater.

I had heard he was in poor health, but was surprised how cachectic and skeletal he had become. Frightening rumors concerning his health had reached me. But when I saw him, I still was not prepared for how he looked. I could see at once he was not going to be with us for very long.

Baldwin was a gracious man. He greeted me warmly, extending his thin fingers in my direction to share a handshake. I felt uncomfortable, as if I were reaching out to greet an old friend whose health was obviously failing—a condition I couldn't easily, or politely, acknowledge.

"Although I still think you should have gotten out on your own long ago, I must thank you for your very kind and generous review of my collections, *The Price of the Ticket* and *The Evidence of Things Not Seen*," I remember him saying to me.

Throughout Baldwin's remarkable career as a writer, teacher, and thinker, there was this terrible consistency. When most writers went in one direction, Baldwin invariably went in another to find a place of intellectual and psychic comfort and to examine carefully his own tough conclusions.

None of this suggests he was totally confident about his life and his work. Indeed, he had doubts and had to come to terms with the fact that during the final years of his existence his reputation as a writer was less than it had been. Other black writers had found acceptance, and Baldwin, for some, had become passé, his anger and bitterness was boring and counterproductive. They charged he had been blinded by his anger toward those who continued their oppression of him and his people.

"The rise and fall of one's reputation," he taught me, "is bound to occur.

"What can you do about it? I think that comes with the territory. A book has its own life. Any real artist will never be judged in the time of his time; whatever judgment of him that is delivered then cannot be trusted," he said.

His eclipse in the marketplace hardly went unnoticed. He handled it well, and never attempted to deny it.

"I'm very vulnerable to all of that," he admitted. "But after all, that's not what it's all about. A book has a season, and it's a great mistake to think you can write a bestseller once a year. The book behind you is the book behind you; the book ahead of you is the book ahead of you. And a success can be as difficult to survive as a failure. When you're a success, if you believe it, you're finished," said Baldwin, a master teacher and talented craftsman who lived a richly creative life—and then moved on.

He Led the Way

Claude Lewis

**He rose to the top
in journalism, then
reached back to
help others.**

The death of Robert Maynard in August 1993 rekindled in my mind several distant memories of him. One of them occurred back in April 1968 when, as young reporters, we traveled to Memphis to cover the tragic and calamitous slaying of the Rev. Dr. Martin Luther King, Jr.

King had arrived in Memphis to support the sanitation workers' strike. The evening before our arrival, he made a startling prophetic speech, reflecting on the likelihood of his early demise.

He had received a greater number of death threats than usual and he spoke about the rampant rumors:

> *Some began to say the threats—or talk about the threats that were . . . out. Or what would happen to me . . . from some of our sick white brothers.*
>
> *Well, I don't know what will happen now. We've got some difficult days ahead. But it really doesn't matter . . . with me now because I've been to . . . the mountain top. I won't mind.*
>
> *Like anybody, I would like to live a long life. Longevity has its*

place. But I'm not concerned about that . . . now. I just want to do God's will.

And he's allowed me to go up to the mountain. And I've looked over, and I've seen the promised land. I may not get there with you but I . . . want you to know tonight that we as a people will get to the promised land.

So I'm happy tonight. I'm not worried about anything. I'm not fearing . . . any man. Mine eyes have seen the glory of the coming of the Lord.

The next evening, as King leaned over a balcony railing outside his room—306—at the Lorraine Motel in downtown Memphis, a bullet crossed a field of wild grass and dead trees and ripped away half of the thirty-nine-year-old Baptist minister's face. King's arms flew upward as he fell back, blood splashing from his neck wound like water rushing from a faucet.

Several of his closest aides arrived to help, but Dr. King was gone. The news of his death stunned the nation and precipitated violent rebellions in major cities across America.

That evening Bob Maynard, then a young *Washington Post* reporter, Earl Caldwell, a member of the staff of the *New York Times*, and I, at that time a reporter for the now defunct *Philadelphia Bulletin*, were at the Lorraine Motel. Police, FBI, and other investigators were everywhere. Chaos reigned.

Maynard drove me to the Western Union office to file my story on the investigation into the assassination of King. The Western Union clerk refused to send the story about a white suspect in the killing of Dr. King. We argued a bit. Then she told me she had already put in a call to "Tom."

"Who's Tom?" I demanded.

"He's our local cop," she huffed, her face red with anger. I thought for a moment and realized that in all probability, Tom would immediately take her side in a dispute with me, a black stranger from the North and a newspaper man at that.

I grabbed my copy and stormed out the door back into the Memphis heat. When I told Bob what had taken place inside the Western Union office, he looked at me with those fiercely penetrating eyes.

"Claude, this is Memphis, Tennessee, 1968. This place is filled with tension and hate. The nation is alive with anger. You'd better get in the car," Maynard said without raising his voice.

"But I'll blow my deadline," I protested.

"Claude, you may blow your deadline, but that cop may blow our heads off. Get in the car."

"If these folks will kill Martin, why would they hesitate to beat or kill us?" he reasoned as I slammed the car door.

Throughout his life, Maynard remained thoroughly logical. He possessed a rich and resonating voice. He used it like a finely tuned instrument. His speech had been measured and firm. People responded to the command quality inherent in his voice, as they did to his words.

Now he was silent, almost pensive as he gunned the motor of the rented car, adroitly executed a U-turn in the small street, and drove hurriedly toward the Lorraine Motel. I kept my eyes on the rearview mirror, hoping that Tom was nowhere in sight.

By the time we reached the Lorraine, it was crowded with reporters from all over the world. Several of them were crammed into my room on the ground floor of the hotel. Some became angry when I told them how the Western Union operator refused to file my story.

Many were in a hostile mood, stemming from Dr. King's murder. One female reporter suggested we go back to Western Union en masse. Maynard realized the folly of that and worked quickly to cool everybody down. Suddenly, his dark face was split by a mischievous smile, and his eyes sparkled.

"Maybe," Maynard kidded aloud, "the operator read your copy and decided it was badly written. Maybe she didn't like your lead."

A dozen frowns turned into puzzled glances that were followed by smiles and then open laughter.

"Maybe the woman decided it wasn't worth the trouble," Maynard deadpanned.

We all had a good laugh and the tension subsided. Maynard had a great sense of humor, and often used his relaxed style to keep things in perspective.

The reports of his death, from cancer, at fifty-six, in the summer of '93, stunned a lot of his friends and colleagues. Bob had announced as much as a year earlier, he was battling prostate cancer. He had always seemed so indestructible and no one who knew him even imagined that he wouldn't win his fight.

He was a good reporter and writer, but he was a far better salesman. He spent his professional life making newspapers better by selling white editors and media executives on the idea that African-Americans and other minorities could function in their newsrooms. Naturally, some resisted his efforts. But Maynard possessed a very special grace.

He and his wife, Nancy Hicks, a former science writer with the *New York Times*, founded the Institute for Journalism Education at Berkeley and helped prepare hundreds of young men and women to enter the profession.

Old arguments that editors could not find "qualified" blacks to function as reporters and editors disappeared quickly, thanks to the efforts of the two of them.

Bob was an unusually articulate and elegant man who found it easy to convince students, sometimes plagued by self-doubt, that they could do the job: "You don't have to be a genius to be a journalist," he counseled.

"If you're willing to do the necessary work, you can be among the best in your profession," Maynard insisted. Indeed, many of his former students are counted among the best.

At sixteen, Maynard dropped out of his Bedford-Stuyvesant high school in Brooklyn. But years later he won a Nieman Fellowship and became one of the best-known journalists in America.

He and his wife spent years teaching minorities—African-Americans, Hispanics, Asians—and women the basics of reporting and writing.

He was the spark plug who kept the engine running. He developed the funding for newspaper projects and pushed his students nearly beyond their endurance to do first-rate jobs.

Late in his career he appeared, with some degree of regularity, on the highly respected ABC-TV Sunday morning television show "This Week with David Brinkley." Always cool, always collected, Bob traded barbs and analysis with Sam Donaldson, George Will, and invited guests and deported himself in the same confident manner that helped make him such an extraordinary member of his profession. Right to the end, he taught his students best by his sterling example.

He crisscrossed the country recruiting potential journalists, making speeches and visiting schools to urge young writers to respect journalism and themselves. He convinced young women that their time had come, that they would be wise to prepare themselves to walk through those newsroom doors that had finally been opened, despite some initial reluctance.

Maynard could give a pep talk at a banquet, hold court in a noisy subway car, or convince people to try things his way. He was proud of his accomplishments and watched with a fatherly pride as many of his students climbed the ladder of success in newspaper and broadcast journalism.

Maynard was good at convincing others because, as a young man, he had some of the same doubts about his own ability. He had come a long way. He began his job as a reporter on the *York Gazette and Daily Record*, in the mountains of southern Pennsylvania. He moved on to the *Washington Post* where he was a reporter and covered several riots for the *Post* before becoming an editor and then later the newspaper's ombudsman.

In 1979, Maynard was named editor of the floundering *Oakland Tribune*. Four years later, using other people's money, namely that of the Gannett Foundation, the Maynards bought the paper and valiantly struggled to keep it afloat.

In his spare time, Bob wrote a syndicated column. However, failing health, mounting bills at the newspaper, and tough union negotiations forced him to sell the paper he had grown to love and which won its first Pulitzer Prize on his watch.

Earl Caldwell said it simply after Maynard's death: "He was

among the very best. Bob did a lot to improve journalism. Newsrooms are far more diverse today with African-Americans, Hispanics, Asians, and women working as reporters, editors, and photographers.

"Bob led the way," Caldwell said, then added thoughtfully, "the greatest tribute I can say about his professionalism is that Bob Maynard is a permanent part of journalism history."

Few would disagree.

Michael H. Cottman

NEW YORK NEWSDAY

Dad

I stood on the steps of St. Mark's Community Church on 12th Street holding my mother's hand, my eyes stinging from the smoke.

I was eleven years old and my father, Howard, had gone for the car while policemen raided an after-hours joint across the street. Helicopters were hovering over the neighborhood and police were shouting through bullhorns, some of them snatching pistols from their holsters. Buildings and houses were beginning to burn and mobs of angry young men raced through the streets. Any questions I had were silenced by sirens.

It was a steamy Sunday in Detroit, July 1967. I was a young witness to the first hours of a week-long riot that today remains a prototype for racial rebellion.

The pews inside the church sanctuary were nearly empty that morning. Most members of the congregation had driven home to avoid any violence. Police were trying to cordon off the area, and several parishioners wondered aloud if the church would soon be consumed by flames.

Rather than leave with the others, my father decided that we should stay, if only briefly, and pray for peace. My father liked this neighborhood, a mixture of black working-class and middle-class families where small shops offered lay-away plans, where neighbors spoke to each other from their porches on summer weekends, car-pooled to work just for company, and kept an extra set of keys to the house next door for emergencies.

It was important for my father to pray for a swift resolution to the riots, but he was also concerned about abandoning this neighborhood—and its residents—in times of trouble. So it was important for us to stay and support my dad.

Following an abbreviated service, my father told my mother and I to wait in front of the church and that he would return with the car, which was parked about a block away. I watched my father walk down the street, turn a corner, and vanish into the confusion. I wanted to run after him but my size 9 feet, tied inside stiff, hard-soled shoes, wouldn't budge.

As the sirens grew louder, the grip of my mother's hand tightened. I had a bad feeling inside. I was afraid that my father wasn't coming back. For the first time in my young life, I thought this was going to be the last time that I was going to see him.

This was, after all, the man who taught me how to ride a bike without training wheels, the man who took me to my first NFL football game, the man who escorted me backstage to hang out with the Four Tops and who took me to the Fox Theater to see a skinny kid named Stevie Wonder blow miraculous music through a harmonica.

This was the man who took me to work with him during the summers, to movies on weekends, a man who always stopped whatever he was doing to help me sort out a problem no matter how small or how monumental. If he didn't have an immediate answer to one of my many questions, he'd take me to the library where we would research the information and find the answer together. I cannot recall a time in my life when my father promised me something and failed to come through. I cannot remember a time when he was supposed to pick me up and was late or never showed up.

He was always there.

Not long after my father disappeared around the corner, a small green car pulled up in front of the church. Much to my relief, he climbed out, opened the door, and ushered my mother and me inside the vehicle. Staring from the backseat of our 1965 Corvair as we turned off 12th Street, I was only happy that my father was alive and driving us home.

That evening, we could hear gunshots in the distance, and later, my father told me that while rushing back to pick us up from the church, he had watched a gang of young boys drag an elderly man from his shoe shop and stomp him to death.

He tried to explain to me why black people were so angry. He didn't condone the violence, but told me about the inequities in the system, how black communities were decaying from neglect and how black people were suffering economically from discrimination. He said that white politicians would respond only to pressure through protests and demonstrations, that discussions and letters were not having much of an impact.

He kissed me good night, as he did every night, reminding me that God listens to my prayers, and hugged me tightly. I felt as if he kept a watchful eye over me all night long—just as he has done every night from a distance since I left home more than twenty years ago.

On any given day inside our home in Detroit, jazz and classical music reverberated throughout the living room where my father still plays recordings of his favorite jazz musicians—Billie Holiday, Duke Ellington, Dizzy Gillespie, Charlie Parker, Billy Eckstine, Dexter Gordon, Sarah Vaughn, Lester Young, and J. C. Heard.

Dad would drink orange juice and offer verbal snapshots of each of these artists; how they got started in their music careers, where they were born, their philosophies on life, the instruments they played, and the other instruments that could be heard in a band. We'd sit and listen to the music and I'd dissect the sounds: a tenor saxophone from an alto sax, drum brushes from drumsticks, a trumpet from a trombone.

My father has always loved music, classical and jazz. His mother, Myron, would call my father and his two sisters into the living room and play the classical masters—Beethoven, Tchaikovsky, and Brahms—on their RCA Victrola each Sunday evening in their home in Indianapolis, Indiana.

But it was the jazz concerts back in 1936—where my father

would stand on the bandstand tiers to observe the techniques of drummers like Chick Webb—that introduced him to the passion of band music. He heard great entertainers like Duke Ellington at clubs on Indiana Avenue, the premiere strip for black businesses and entertainment.

Dad would talk to me about how many of these musicians excelled despite pervasive racial discrimination in the music industry.

Dad knew something about jazz—and he knew something about racism.

In 1943, during World War II, my father joined the Army–Air Force, as it was then called. He was stationed at a base in Greensboro, North Carolina, one of many segregated Army installations across the country.

Dad played drums in an all-black band that entertained troops on and off the base. It was through his music and the band that he met and played with tenor saxophone player James Moody and a host of other talented African-American men who decided to pursue a career in music after their discharge. While stationed in Greensboro, my father became buddies with Dizzy Gillespie, who he met in 1945 after a show that included the Nicholas Brothers and June Eckstine.

My father and Dizzy became fast friends, and Dad followed Dizzy's career for over fifty years. Dad met Dizzy for beers each time the jazz musician played Detroit or Chicago. They spent hours talking into the night after the sets.

When Dizzy died in 1993, the world lost an extraordinary jazz musician—but my father lost a close friend. The last time my father saw Dizzy was Friday night, May 3, 1991, inside the Attic Theater, a popular jazz club on the west side of Detroit. After scores of people filed down the three aisles to the stage where Dizzy signed autographs, the house lights dimmed shortly before midnight and Dizzy and my father sat on the corner of the stage. They talked about old times, old tunes, and a friendship that had spanned five decades.

The United States military was the first and only white organization that my father ever worked for full-time. It was an experience that didn't make him bitter, but it did strengthen his belief that African-Americans should establish our own businesses, patronize existing black businesses and help rebuild black communities while grooming our own business and political leaders.

He devoted forty years to black businesses and many more to the black church. After he was discharged from the Army–Air Force, my father worked in sales at the *Michigan Chronicle*, Detroit's black newspaper and the Great Lakes Life Insurance Company, Detroit's first black-owned insurance company.

Several years later, he joined the sales and marketing division of the Johnson Publishing Co. (*Ebony/Jet*), and after being wooed by Johnson Products Co. (Ultra Sheen Afro-Sheen), he accepted the job. He served as a consultant with M&M Products (Sta-Sof-Fro) before he retired. He was part of the country's first generation of black white-collar workers, preferring to use his mind instead of his hands.

While I was in high school, my father talked a lot about corporate America, having read the biographies of Henry Ford, Lee Iacocca, and other wealthy CEOs. He explained the realities of discrimination in American society and talked about how life as a black man in the workplace would pose certain challenges and uncertainties. He told me never to compromise my integrity, to stand up for issues that I believed in and to speak out if I felt that I was being discriminated against.

He prepared me for the feeling of isolation while working in corporate America, the times when I have been the only African-American in the newsroom, or when there have been few African-Americans making key decisions at the newspaper.

Never quite satisfied with the African-American history that I was being taught in grade school, my father would supplement those lessons with teachings of his own. He would take me to African-American history museums and buy me books about black history and African culture.

He encouraged me to write and made sure that I was exposed to some of the greatest black writers of our time: Frederick Douglass, Ralph Ellison, James Baldwin, Richard Wright, and Langston Hughes. He talked about the importance of African-Americans telling our own stories and documenting our own history. He would clip newspaper articles for me to read about successful black businessmen and women in Detroit and, more important, he would take me to meet them.

Conversations with my father became more intense as I got older. He repeatedly told me that I could accomplish anything in life, that I would only be limited by my own imagination and lack of tenacity. It was just the psychological foundation I needed, growing up in Detroit where some of my boyhood buddies ended up on drugs or dead. Peer pressure was mounting and my dad saw young black boys destroying their lives through crime and the fathering of illegitimate children.

Times were changing. The bats and sticks that were used for weapons in schoolyard fights were being replaced with guns and knives. The violence from civil unrest was real. I had already seen one riot and felt the psychological damage while watching the physical destruction. I didn't know then that as a newspaper reporter I would end up covering three major riots—two in Miami and one in the Crown Heights section of Brooklyn.

To escape the escalation of crime, we moved to a predominantly white suburb of Detroit in my senior year of high school where, ironically, drugs were more accessible than at any school I had attended in Detroit. Today that neighborhood is predominantly black.

In our new home, my father would talk to me about the responsibility that comes with growing up, the responsibility that comes with being a black man: treating black women with respect, never calling them "bitches," and never raising my hand to hit a woman.

But the one issue that my father brought up most was being responsible about sex. He warned me about the consequences of recklessly bringing children into the world and recalled how many black men were fathering children they couldn't afford and didn't want. If I did get someone pregnant, he told me one evening before dinner, then I would take responsibility for the woman and the child; that there would be no walking away from a family that was my own.

He couldn't have been more serious.

My father learned his respect for women at a young age from

his mother, his role model, Myron Cottman. She taught him about the fortitude of black women by her example: raising three children (my father and his two sisters) while working every day and caring for my grandfather, Howard Sr., for eighteen months until he died when my father was only five years old.

Dad's mother worked early days and late nights for little money, but still, as a single parent, made ends meet: she paid the bills, had hot food on the table every morning and evening, washed clothes for the children, and gave them change for the collection plate at church.

She made sure that my father and his sisters avoided "The Corner"—a grungy hangout one block from their home—where unemployed men would stand outside a liquor store drinking half-pints of whiskey, gamble, and lust after young girls.

My grandmother had a profound and lasting influence on my father's life. He watched a strong black woman provide for a busy household and, at the end of the day, still muster enough energy to check homework and read bedtime stories. During that time, children were being sent to orphanages because their parents couldn't afford to take care of them. Love, she would tell my father, was the one ingredient that would keep their family together.

Too often in America, young black boys are without fathers to talk to them about responsibility—and about the strength of black women and the admiration they deserve.

One afternoon, on April 4, 1968, I came in from the playground to find my father sitting in front of our black-and-white television, his eyes red from tears. I knew something terrible had happened. He told me that Martin Luther King, Jr., had been shot and killed in Memphis, that he was murdered because he spoke out on behalf of black people and that the world had lost a great leader who stood for peace.

I cried, too, but not for King. I cried because I had never seen my father so devastated by a single event. He was bothered by the violent direction of the country. He had witnessed the shoe shop owner being killed the year before, a graphic image he never forgot. He was struck by how callously someone can take a human life. With few words on the day that King was murdered, my father taught me that showing emotion does not make a man weak. It makes a man human. It makes a man spiritually stronger. It makes him honest.

On one recent visit to Detroit, I sat at the kitchen table while my father scrambled eggs and strained oranges for freshly squeezed juice. We talked about how the campaign by House Republicans to repeal the country's affirmative action policies was an orchestrated effort to further lock African-Americans out of the workplace and polarize an already racially torn society.

We talked about how white males have created an illusion that African-Americans have displaced them in the workplace despite no statistical proof to support their complaints and how white males who make up a third of the country's population, make up 80 percent of Congress, nine-tenths of the Senate, four-fifths of the tenured university faculty, and 92 percent of the *Forbes* 400. My father insists that without legal pressure white men will continue to hire those who look like themselves.

My father, who is seventy-seven years old, says those statistics —and the racial attitudes that produce them—are not likely to change during his lifetime.

I'm not a father yet, but I hope to be one someday. I don't know if I'll make a great father, but I do know what makes a father great: never missing a son's birthday, father-and-son banquets at church, unannounced visits to your son's school, exposing him to swimming, horseback riding, arts and science, pulling him aside to whisper wise words on his wedding day, sending him books, and every now and again, telling your son that you're proud of him.

Perhaps my father embraces me with the spirit of his Dad— the father that he never really had an opportunity to know.

My relationship with my father and the respect that I have for him is not unique in our community. But it is special. No, he doesn't slam-dunk basketballs in the NBA, he doesn't rap on stage, and he has never been featured in a music video.

But my father is my one true role model.

And even as I close in on my fortieth year, my father still

serves me a plate of scrambled eggs and reminds me that I can come to him for anything, anytime. He will always be there for me just as he was on that sweltering summer morning nearly thirty years ago as I watched a social revolution forge a conflicted path for a generation of young black men. And I'm convinced that if I follow in his footsteps, they will always lead me home.

Dorothy Gilliam

WASHINGTON POST

Crossroads to Africa

Teach us, Forever Dead,
there is no Dream but
Deed, there is no Deed
but Memory.
—*W. E. B. Du Bois*

I wanted to see the sun-kissed shores of Africa.

In my father's African Methodist Episcopal Church in Louisville, Kentucky, I learned from bishops who'd spent time in Africa of a people far different from the images of Tarzan, Jane, and savages that I saw on the screen of the Lyric Theater.

The simmering fire of curiosity was ignited when I was a student at Lincoln University, a historically black college in Jefferson City, Missouri, in the late 1950s. While I had learned about black history and achievement in Kentucky, it was in the classes of Dr. Lorenzo Greene that a new sense of pride was born as he stripped away shrouds of distortion and strove to accurately mirror the past. "Black history did not begin with slavery," Dr. Greene, perched on the edge of his desk, intoned earnestly.

Still, as human nature would have it, it was my budding friendship with a brilliant young Kenyan trade unionist and political leader named Tom Mboya, who I got to know on his frequent trips to America, that further piqued my interest in seeing the continent.

The chance to turn fantasy into reality came when I was at the

Columbia University Graduate School of Journalism in the early 1960s. I learned of a program started by a black Harlem minister that took U.S. students to Africa for a summer to live and work with African students. Not only was I accepted and encouraged to go by the Rev. James Robinson, founder of the program called Operation Crossroads Africa that was the model for the Peace Corps, but I was steered to sources of money to help defray the costs.

For several years before my first trip to Africa, I had intermittently struggled for self-esteem and self-assurance in the white world I'd entered after I left the protected black cocoon in which I grew up. My first experience was as one of nine young black women who integrated a small white Catholic women's college in Louisville. Two years later, I transferred to Lincoln University to study journalism. At Columbia, I was one of two blacks and the only black woman in my class. Before taking a job (I hoped) at a mainstream newspaper, I thought a trip to Africa would be an important boost to my morale.

I was frightened as our plane touched down in Lagos, Nigeria. What would I find? Walking into the airport, I was shocked to see so many black people in positions of responsibility. Everybody who was doing anything was black—police officers, airline ticket agents, customs officials, and skycaps.

What an awakening! White America told black Americans that segregation was justified in part because blacks were not capable of certain tasks. We always knew we could do more than society told us and my entire upbringing had been a strong counterattack against this vile offensive. Yet a little tape in my brain must have recorded some of the lies. Even though my church, school, family, and community told me that I could do almost anything I set my mind to and helped me prepare to do just that, I must have had secret doubts whether blacks were the equal of whites even as the civil rights movement was rocking America's equilibrium.

My amazement continued on the ride from the airport to Lagos—it was exhilarating just to see so many black people. Market women on the side of the road, people walking, riding bikes and buses, honking car horns. It was with some satisfaction that the black Crossroaders heard about some of their white counterparts, who had to be sent back to America because they couldn't take the culture shock of an all-black country. They found being a tiny minority too overwhelming.

After Lagos, the larger group broke down into smaller ones to travel to different countries. My group of eighteen included fifteen whites and three blacks and was headed by a black professor from Atlanta. We headed to Kenya.

Although the winds of change were blowing, Kenya in the early 1960s was still a favored colony of the English people. An incredibly beautiful land of high altitude, mountains, clean fresh air, temperate climate, and exotic animals, the Nairobi area was home of the White Highlands, the most beautiful part of Kenya, where the English lived primarily on estates and farms.

The Africans lived in various settings. The Kikuyu, for example, lived as squatters on farms on European-held land in various districts, on their own reserves, and in the towns. As agriculturists, the Kikuyu herded animals, which were essential to their social organization.

For years, the Kenyans, under the leadership of Jomo Kenyatta, had staged a guerrilla movement for freedom known as Mau. While Kenyatta had been jailed and banned, men like Tom Mboya were involved in very delicate negotiations for his freedom with the British while fighting political and tribal battles at home. Kenyatta's release was rumored to occur during the summer we were in Kenya.

Our group's task was to build a road from the highway back to a children's hospital that was being built seven miles outside of Nairobi, the capital city. We slept on cots in tents, sharing them with our African counterparts, took cold showers, and drank lots of English tea.

The Crossroaders were predominantly from Harvard and Radcliffe, who bought with them some stereotypical thinking about Africans; subsequently, cultural problems emerged. For instance, some of them thought the Africans didn't work hard enough. I remember looking at them and saying, "Look at you. How many vitamins have you taken in your life? How many doctors have you been to to prevent your having childhood diseases and dentists to give you braces? You sit down and drink a quart of milk at a meal. You're criticizing people who haven't—and don't have—the same diet and advantages you have."

Being in Africa was marvelous, frightening, frustrating, and infuriating. One day, two white Crossroaders and I tried to hitchhike into Nairobi. We stood on the highway with our thumbs out and white settlers would see my two white companions and slow down. But when they saw me as well, they'd hit the accelerator, saying, "We can take YOU two but we can't pick HER up." I felt the same way I felt when a cab refused to pick me up in New York or Washington.

I felt the fury rise up in me repeatedly as I stood there thinking of my early romantic notions of "going home." In Nigeria, the colonialists had played a more behind-the-scenes role, but whites in Kenya were as prejudiced as I imagined they were in England. Here I was in Africa, I fumed, and the horrible hand of white supremacy was still on our backs.

Happily, the Africans' excitement about independence coated such bitter pills. On the highways and side roads, we saw old women, bent low with loads of wood—held on their backs by leather straps, which they hitched around their foreheads—lift their fingers and make the victory sign. "Uhuru, Uhuru," ("Freedom" in Swahili) they shouted. So poor in material things, they were rich in spirit and noticeably anxious to bring to an end England's colonial rule of their country.

Meanwhile, my little *affaire la coeur* was hitting stony ground as I realized the naïveté behind my infatuation with Mboya. Despite our frequent meetings in Nairobi, it was an eye-opening experience for a twenty-three-year-old Kentucky girl to recognize that there was no possibility that Mboya, with his dreams of one day being president of Kenya, would get deeply involved with an American, even a black one. Given the tribal rivalries that dominated Kenya, it was clear that he would end up with an African woman who could be his political helpmate in more ways than one. He married a fellow Luo several years later.

I sated my disappointment by plotting to meet Jomo Kenyatta. Near the end of our three-month stay, when we'd completed three separate construction projects, the word came down that Kenyatta was going to be released from detention and freed to his compound at Gatundi. Another Crossroader, Emily Schrader, of Radcliffe, and I decided to be inside the compound to have a front-row seat on history. We offered to help the women unpack the dishes and clean the house that had been unoccupied for some time.

The excitement was incredible. Kenyatta not only symbolized freedom, he was idolized by many Kenyans as the father of independence, the man who was restoring their country to them. For days before his release, people began lining up on the roads leading to his house—sleeping on the sides of the roads, in fields, and in cars—just to glimpse him when he drove by. The high-pitched sound the women made in celebration and welcome—a cry of joy—filled the air for days, rolling around the countryside.

Finally, his car appeared down the road. He was dressed in pants and a loose-fitting shirt, no palatial ceremonial robes. As he arrived on the grounds, politicians, government and union leaders, and ordinary people as well stepped up to greet him. And nearby I stood among the throngs, smiling in wonderment at being on the scene the day Jomo Kenyatta strode to freedom.

3

Glimpses of the Past

Larry Whiteside

BOSTON GLOBE

Double Duty

s a kid growing up on the South Side of Chicago in the late 1940s, I always wanted to play baseball in the Negro Leagues. Don't laugh. There are still a few of us left. I speak of when Negroes, as we were called then, worshiped few men of color. Joe Lewis was the greatest. My father said he first saw Satchel Paige in 1928, when he was eighteen years old. They were the best black athletes in a sports world dominated by whites.

Black baseball was for a black youngster of that era the only real baseball. If you couldn't afford the price of a ticket to "Watermelon Heaven" at Comiskey Park, as the black-dominated bleachers were called, you hiked down the road to 53rd and South Parkway. If times were good, you hopped a jitney cab for a dime. Once there, beyond a cluster of woods that was interrupted by a public debate area where the Negro from slavery to Paul Robeson was discussed, you'd see one of the several Negro League playing fields. A real Field of Dreams. Black Dreams.

If you went to "The Park" today, you'd see a grassy plain suitable for sun-drenched picnics, and children wandering off for hours. Forty years ago, when the Negro Leagues were in their heyday, it was midtown haven, green grass and long rows of trees, surrounding several cozy little coves. This was the home of the Chicago American Giants, or the Black Knights of Baseball, as we chose to call them. No castle in fairyland could have been better.

Perched high in a tree, I could see the whole field. It mattered not to me that some of the uniforms were tattered, and not all matched. Hell, the players' shucking and jiving was the only way to talk, I thought. I wanted to be like them. I wanted to pitch like Satchel. I wanted to run like Cool Papa Bell. I thought I could hit and catch like Josh Gibson. I could say all of this because, except for excursions to "The Park," I had never seen these Black Knights perform on a big league diamond, and thus everything I wished for was possible. It was only later in life that I discovered there was more than met the eyes; that these were grown men playing a kid's game, and not the other way around.

I began to learn this the summer of 1947. How I got Alonzo Whiteside, Sr., to take his youngest son to Comiskey Park, I'll never know. I was ten the following year when he took me to see the 1948 Negro League All-Star game, and I saw wondrous things I have never forgotten. I was in a crowd of 48,112, mostly black baseball fans. Forty years later, I have yet to feel again the emotions that went through me that day. On the field, I saw powerful but somehow agile black men pound the small white baseball, and with each hit, each toss around the diamond, I was proud. I saw Josh Gibson, Minnie Minoso, Quincy Troupe, Goose Tatum, Monte Irvin, Luis Tiant, Sr., Sam Jethro, and Dan Bankhead. Later, I asked my father why these men weren't playing against the Cubs and the White Sox, if they were so good. It took years for me to understand why he couldn't answer.

It was on this day that I began to learn about life as well as baseball. Neither was ever meant to be perfect. Purists will tell you racism still survives, and the game has moved very little since opening its doors in 1947. But we've come a long way since those days, and fortunately for the men of the Negro Leagues, it is a full circle. A couple of years ago I was party to a wondrous change, and at all places, Cooperstown, New York, home to the Baseball Hall of Fame. A miracle happened. Major League

Baseball found a way to pay homage to the men of a great era and a great league, without feeling either a sense of shame or a loss of dignity. For the last three decades you could visit Cooperstown and find some Negro League inductees, a total of eleven at last count. But this was a formal gesture, with no heart for the people who were Major League Baseball outcasts from 1900 to 1947. But in the summer of 1991, when seventy players and their families showed up as invited guests of a game that once shunned them, it wrote an end to a chapter of baseball history that could have been nothing but bitterness for as long as these men live. It didn't mean a lot to the modern baseball world. But it did to me. It gave me renewed faith in the Black Knights of my youth. They are still my greatest sports heroes. It is not their fault that the history books have been slow in recording their remarkable deeds and lifestyles.

With this in mind, I must tell you of Ted (Double Duty) Radcliffe, pushing his nineties, last I heard. Like a lot of the people who showed up in Cooperstown, he kept wondering out loud why it took them so long. The Black Knights never had all that much. But nobody was ever going to take away their pride, least of all some white boys they used to beat regularly back in the good old days. Jackie Robinson might have been a lightweight if he'd been forced to stay in the Negro Leagues.

"People talk about the Negro League and segregation," said Double Duty, who sat in the lobby of the Ontegsage Hotel and held court for several hours. In his thirty-six-year career, he was a catcher and a pitcher for half a dozen teams. Later, he was a manager and knew more about what was going on than most folks.

"Most places we went, we always had the respect of the white players. They were very nice because they made money with us. When I first started playing against Lefty Grove, he wasn't making more than $10,000 a year. The average guy was making around $3,500. Heck, they weren't making any more than me.

"People ask us all the time if we are bitter. I tell them we didn't think about it, really, until the fifties when Martin Luther King, Jr., started the fight for integration. Before, it didn't do no good. It didn't get you anywhere. We didn't care about making money in those days. We loved baseball. I had all the gals I wanted. So that was enough."

When I went to that All-Star game with my father, he was trying to explain to me that in the Negro Leagues, I was seeing the cream of the black and Latin talent. I thought that it was just American-born Negroes who were suffering. By 1954, when the doctrine of separate but equal was cut down by the courts, I would understand that this was something these men shared with all people of color, who were denied opportunities because of the tint of their skin. To be the best, and be denied a chance at something because of race was just not fair. As the years went by, I saw this change happen in law, medicine, and education. The Negro Leagues just led the way. I would also come to understand that while the self-contained lifestyle of many black Americans had its faults, to be sure, things weren't always going to be bad. The Negro Leagues taught us it was okay to be black and live black. We could still be first class and never have to spend one day begging for a hot meal or a place to stay, unless we really wanted.

I miss the Negro Leagues, but it helps to know they had a role in shaping baseball history. In 1947, when the color line was broken by Jackie Robinson, it crumbled under the weight of a nation awakening to an untapped resource. Baseball was suffering without black men—sixteen all-white teams in two leagues, with pro football and pro basketball on the verge of challenging their dominance. After Jackie Robinson, baseball became the dominant sport for the next four decades. While the Negro Leagues faded into a sad memory, the immediate descendants changed the direction of the game. Some, like Ernie Banks, Willie Mays, Hank Aaron, and Monte Irvin, walked through the palace gates. But if you believe in God, like most blacks, you know he does not abandon his "chosen people." The rest of them are just coming along. Thus a tiny reunion, first in 1989 in Louisville, Kentucky, had helped bring back the Negro Leagues' legends stronger than in the thirties and forties. And in the years since then, a once insensitive white and black public has come to realize what a giant debt we owe to the owners and players of these black baseball teams. Need a Kansas City Monarchs T-shirt? It's available along with the Homestead Grays, the New York Cubans, and half a dozen others from Negro League teams. The legends of their players now grow, not diminish.

Personally, Jackie Robinson will always be my ultimate role model. But recently I found myself thinking about Double Duty, and what he said about the Negro Leagues. He's my hero, too. He taught me that the Negro Leaguers were real black people, not a group of dancing gypsies as depicted in *The Bingo Long Traveling All-Stars & Motor Kings*. Double Duty might not be the best example of Negro League manhood. He was a rascal who didn't mind putting a sexual connotation to his unique nickname. But he talked about the things the Negro Leagues were about. Now at least once a year Major League Baseball teams honor the stars of old Negro Leagues, proud black men in their seventies and eighties, dressed "clean to the bone."

The *Bingo Long All-Stars* movie is a joke, Radcliffe and other Negro League veterans remind us. It ignores the fact that the great black players could have played for any team in baseball. In fact, in the late 1920s and most of the 1930s, the Negro League teams often played clubs made up of mostly major league talent, and beat them regularly. The movie seemed to suggest that the Negro League men were of low moral fiber, and perhaps drank too much . . . everyday. Don't ever say that in front of a true Negro Leaguer. Many were college graduates, including Jackie Robinson. They were family men. Many had successful second careers, which paid much more money than a black baseball player earned. Most of the great players of the thirties and forties have already been elevated to the Hall of Fame, courtesy of the Veteran Committee of the Baseball Writers Association of America. But some of the so-called ordinary ones would be there, too, had the color line dropped in the thirties and not the forties.

"People are quick to point out what Jackie Robinson went through," said Radcliffe. "Hell, he didn't have it any worse than us. We had to go into the back of a grocery store to get baloney. I was glad he got a break. Sorry it wasn't me. When he went up, I was around forty-three. They weren't going to take me at that age."

And if you wanted to know about the ageless one.

"Satchel was born July 7, 1900," insists Radcliffe. "I know because I was born July 7, 1902, and we lived four blocks apart. I started to catch for him when I was fifteen. We used to play on a semi-pro team for a quarter so that we could go to the show [movies]."

For years, when I sought information about the Negro Leagues, I leaned on my bible, a book entitled *Only the Ball Was White*. I knew the Red Sox were the last major league team to bring a black player to the majors. I found out by reading the book that Piper Davis, who had played on the same Birmingham Black Baron team as Willie Mays, had been in spring training ten years before that, and never got farther north than Scranton. There is a Negro League museum in Kansas City. Black sports heroes are now showing up everywhere. There are currently eleven Negro League players in the Hall of Fame in Cooperstown, not including Hank Aaron, Ernie Banks, Willie Mays, and Roy Campanella, all of whom had firm roots in Negro League baseball. The absence of Larry Doby is puzzling, but there is still time.

I am reminded that the dream of most Negro League players to one day play in the major leagues was a nightmare for most. Light-skinned Latins showed up in the teens, and again in the thirties. But it wasn't automatic. A dark-skinned superstar from Cuba named Luis Tiant, Sr., never did. He should be in the Hall of Fame one day, too. You have to remember that the color line was just that, a stupid and arbitrary criteria that deprived hundreds of quality athletes from playing what was even then called the Great American game. It never made sense, but it went on for decades until Jackie Robinson broke through. He went to UCLA and was an all-American. But he became a man in the Negro Leagues.

How good were those black boys?

"One year, we played a post-season series with Detroit, and beat them eleven of thirteen games," recalled Double Duty. "After that, the commissioner [Judge Kenesaw Landis] stopped us from barnstorming with any team intact. The next year we beat the Connie Mack All-Stars, and they stopped us from playing altogether. We couldn't play them anymore until he [Landis] died.

"Were we good? Ask the white boys! Ask those barnstormers. We kicked ass every time we played them."

Players of the Negro Leagues are a storehouse of baseball anecdotes that should be cherished rather than forgotten.

The Hall of Fame has no special wing for the Negro Leagues. There is a section on its history, but the names of its members are dotted around the exhibition hall with the regular inductees. No segregation here. They include: Cool Papa Bell, Oscar Charleston, Ray Dandridge, Martin Dihigo, Rube Foster, Josh Gibson, Monte Irvin, Judy Johnson, Buck Leonard, John Lloyd, and Satchel Paige.

Double Duty Radcliffe hasn't made it yet.

"I still tell people about the Homestead Grays of 1931," said Double Duty, who is still hopeful he may be voted into the Hall of Fame. "We had the best players in the world. We won twenty-seven straight that year. We'd have done well against the 1927 Yankees.

"I recall once our bus was going through Waycross, Georgia," said Double Duty. "We stopped the bus to buy some gas. The boys got out to drink some water from a hose used to wash the cars. The owner said, 'Nigger put that hose down. That's for white folks to drink. Get yourself a Coca-Cola bottle.' We refused to buy gas from him, and I was glad. We went four miles down the road and ran out, and had to push it five miles. But we weren't going to buy any gas from him. Or Coca-Cola."

Get it? There are some stories people ought to hear, even if it pushes the limits. I asked Double Duty was if it was true that he threw out Ty Cobb in a barnstorming game in Cuba in 1926? Yes, the same Ty Cobb who ten years earlier had stolen ninety-six bases for the Detroit Tigers.

"Cobb was near the end of his career," recalled Radcliffe, "but he could still run. But also, I had a bullet arm. I could throw the ball one hundred miles an hour. So I threw him out. Not once, but three times. And he left. Before he went, however, he said,

'I'll never play against another nigger team.' I laughed. I wore a sign on my chest when I was young that said, 'Thou Shall Not Steal.' And I meant that."

To preserve these men and their deeds is more than a notion. In 1990, Double Duty was living in Chicago's Ida B. Wells projects, when his world almost came to a premature end. Twice Double Duty and his wife were beaten up, and another time he had his car wrecked by a hoodlum. But with the help from friends in and out of baseball, he survived, moving to a church-owned senior citizens building across the street. There he found safety and peace of mind, and the respect of his neighbors.

"I'm not bitter about anything," says Double Duty. "But when I was at the Hall of Fame, I told them they'd better put me in because time was running out."

Okay, if you must know, Double Duty got his nickname because of a doubleheader at Yankee Stadium in 1931. Satchel pitched and Double Duty caught the first game of the doubleheader, winning 5–0. Double Duty pitched the second game for the Grays, and won 4–0.

"The next day, the boy Damon Runyon gave me the name Double Duty," said Radcliffe. "Been that way ever since."

Howard Bryant

OAKLAND TRIBUNE

Joe Black's Legacy

He was not a star, but a nova, appearing, flaring, and disappearing, each phase following the other so rapidly that before there was time to contemplate one phenomenon it had been succeeded by another.
—*Roger Kahn on Joe Black* (*Boys of Summer*, 1973)

The games are definitely over, yet his work is never done. The sky was a fatigued blurry shade of red as the Arizona sun began to set over his home in Phoenix. As a man, Joe Black could relate.

He wasn't a boxer, but Black is well schooled in the game of defending himself and fighting back. After seven decades, his arms were heavy, weary from the long years of administering and absorbing blows of the battle. As the southwestern air soothed his large frame, Black grew restless.

I last saw Black at the Oakland Coliseum in 1993. He, along with about fifteen other former warriors of the Negro Leagues were being honored before an A's–Kansas City Royals regular season match.

It has been more than thirty-seven years since Joe Black last entered the arena that he called home for about six years. For those not familiar with his work, Joe Black threw lethal fastballs around 94 mph for the Brooklyn Dodgers during the racially charged years of the early 1950s.

As Black sat in the Coliseum, he was soon surrounded by young children, the majority African-American. To these young kids, all clad in the latest sneakers and bright baseball caps, Black was something of an anomaly. So much had changed.

"They really don't know about it, what it was like," Black said of the children who surrounded him.

While Black signed autographs, he asked youngsters what they knew about the turbulent time when Black entered the majors, when African-American participation in the national pastime was at issue. Few could tell him much. But he persisted.

"The important thing is to leave them with a message," he said. "It takes a while for them to understand that picture, that it wasn't an act of cowardice to turn the other cheek."

In the continuum of baseball, he was not a household name. It is probable that most baseball fans do not know of Joe Black's significance. But at age twenty-eight, nearly ancient in baseball terms, Black was named Rookie of the Year in 1952. Winning fifteen games, and saving another fifteen while losing only four, Black went on to be one of the game's best relievers as the Dodgers won the National League pennant. In the first game of the 1952 World Series, Black became the first African-American to win a game in the World Series.

But his is not the story of a brilliant ball player whose superior talent overcame bigotry and race hatred. He was not an immortal, like Willie Mays, whose charisma, power, and skill at times rendered him virtually raceless. To America, and more particularly the baseball world, Joe Black was that precisely: "They didn't make it easy," Black said, shifting his heavy frame. "My name was the ultimate reminder."

Joe Black's year was 1952. After playing in the minor leagues with the Montreal Royals, Black entered the major league fray. The heat of a pennant race wilted many an athlete, but it strengthened Black.

This was not the mere pressure of the pennant race. Athletes thrive in pressure situations with regularity. The derisive cry of "Old Black Joe" from opposing dugouts became a customary greeting when Black entered a game. Against St. Louis, a black cat was thrown on the field when he entered a ball game. In Philadelphia, the Phillies bench would cry "N-I-G-G-E-R" when Black entered a game.

When Jackie Robinson batted against Philadelphia, Ben Chapman, the Phillies manager, yelled at Robinson, questioning how many white women Robinson would chase after the game. Black, along with the rest of the handful of black players, was expected to take the abuse and just play ball.

To combat such aggressions, Black once threw his deadly fastball at the heads of the first seven Cincinnati batters one year, finally putting a stop to the singing. He repeated the act in Chicago.

"They'd be singing 'Old Black Joe' and I'd already be mad. I'd separate a guy's hat from his head with a fastball," he said. "They used to call me and Newk [Dodger pitcher Don Newcombe] the headhunters," he said in 1992. "That used to quiet 'em."

The New York Giants feared him, as did the St. Louis Cardinals. In the World Series, he beat the Yankees in the opener of the '52 Series. Many black pitchers would win World Series games in following years, but fittingly, Joe Black was the first.

Generally, there are two ways to achieve fame in sports: either by enjoying a long, established, and distinguished career or by being at the right place at the right time and making the most of it. Joe Black was the latter. When the game was on the line, Joe Black was not far from the spotlight.

But where there is triumph, anguish cannot be far behind; the symmetry is too great. Heroism was close enough to see, to touch, but it eluded Black's enormous grasp. His luster tarnished. He lost two games in the '52 Series, including a gutsy Game Seven at Ebbets Field. He didn't know it then, but as a ball player, his star had fallen.

And as quickly as his fame arrived, it was over. Black would not win (or pitch particularly well) another post-season game for his career. A weakened arm betrayed him. The fastball, once incendiary, failed him. His curve, a staple of pinpoint control, couldn't find the strike zone. The supreme confidence, which once decked opposing hitters, deserted him.

On June 9, 1955, the Dodgers traded him to Cincinnati. Two years later, after an unsuccessful stint with the old Washington Senators, he was gone, out of baseball.

Black is now seventy years old. His hair is gray with speckles of black. While playing, Black stood an imposing six-foot-two, and weighed in at a muscular but slender 220 pounds. His hair was short, cropped close. Standing on the pitching rubber at Ebbets Field, wearing his Dodger number 49, he was a giant.

He now creaks close to 300 pounds; overweight, but healthy. There is a fire that smolders within him. It isn't the same flame that burned within his biggest hero, Jackie Robinson, but he is still hot to the touch.

Time has been kind to Black. Many of his contemporaries on those old Dodger teams—Roy Campanella, Junior Gilliam, and Jackie Robinson, for example—have passed on. As the men have left, Black fears the lessons learned may also be forgotten.

"He carried us and we tried to follow the example . . . to pass it down the line," Black said of the Robinson influence. The qualities that allowed Black, Bob Gibson, Don Newcombe, Henry Aaron, Robinson, and Mays to survive transcended sport. There was a black pride that came along with being a player as well as a fan.

In many ways, he and his generation are an anachronism. Progress has erased much of what Black and Robinson confronted. But while Black sat surrounded by the anxious pack of children, ranging from six to about twelve or thirteen years old, each one of them looked at him with respect, and tried, as young kids do, to answer his questions. With each incorrect answer, he shook his head. He wasn't merely disappointed, Joe Black was hurt.

What he wanted more than anything else as he signed baseballs for the black kids was for them to answer his questions. He wanted to know that they knew something about this bygone era of black history.

Wearing his old Baltimore Elite Giants jersey, Black spoke to the kids. He didn't like what he was hearing.

"They just don't get it," he said regretfully, a little more spice lacing his husky speech. He is well attuned to the greater truth: that he is one of the few living links to a period in time that in just a few years will forever be a footnote to history.

"They don't have to know who I am, but they should at least know about *him*."

"Him" was Robinson, the brightest symbol of black gallantry and black courage in the history of American sports. Black defers to his hero, in a faint hope the message is not lost.

"You know, people just don't understand what he went through, so that it could be a little easier for the rest of us. He took everything, all the taunts, the death threats, the humiliation. And he took it for all of us."

Hands slightly trembling, Black signed baseball after baseball. Despite the air conditioning, his brow perspired. Black asked the children who their favorite ball players were. The names were modern, and stellar indeed. But it wasn't enough.

"It isn't the same," he said, pained lines etched in his face. He was suddenly dour.

Finally, a girl about eight said that Jackie Robinson was the first black player to play Major League Baseball. She had a slight problem pronouncing the word *integration*.

Maybe the lessons haven't been completely forgotten after all, Joe Black must have thought to himself as he smiled.

Jeff Rivers

HARTFORD COURANT

The Gospel According to Smokey and Curtis

During the early sixties, the old ones would regale me with stories about growing up and working in the fields of their native South.

"Cotton." "Tobacco." They'd say the words as if they could conjure up an entire world long past with the names of those two crops. Cotton and tobacco were short for: "Worked me from sunup to sundown. Worked me like a mule. Worse than a mule. They'd let the mule rest. And white folks were really something else then, man. You think they bad today . . ."

I was a little boy growing up in Philadelphia then. Polite, seen when and where I was supposed to be. Seldom heard. A good boy. The old ones would look at my hands and my long piano-player fingers. They'd say, "Now you don't know nothing about that, do you, son?"

I'd shake my head. They'd smile, glad I didn't know and they clearly hoped I'd never find out. Today, most of the old ones from my childhood are gone. And it's time for me to take their places.

People who don't know any better would say I'm too young to start thinking of myself as one of the old ones. But when I return to the old neighborhood in Philly, I discover that three of my childhood playmates are dead. Another is, at forty, already a grandfather.

Those things make me feel older than my thirty-nine years, make me think I'm ready to be one of the old ones.

So I want to tell the young ones my story. But mine is not a story of hardship or struggle, though there was some of that.

My story is a tale of romance. I want to tell the young ones about singers Smokey Robinson and Curtis Mayfield. When I was growing up, girls and women were treasured. That's what Smokey and Curtis taught us. You wanted to walk the beautiful black women of their songs and of our neighborhoods home. When they kissed you—and that's all most did—they knocked you off your feet. They were sweet and you had to be sweet to win them over. "You look as if you're softer than a rosebud and you're warmer than the sun that makes it grow . . ."

When I was younger, black women made the sun shine. If you were lucky, you had one you could call "my girl." They were all you could talk about. And you wanted to talk about them all the time. "I want to talk about my baby." Yeah, yeah.

Unfortunately, unless they listen to the oldies stations, the young ones don't know anything about the world of romance, the world Curtis and Smokey wrote and sang about, the world I came of age in.

I want to tell the young ones that when I was a younger man, the most beautiful woman in the world walked me to a bus stop. It was winter. Snow fell. But it was not cold. My bus drew close. The woman kissed me.

I sang Smokey all the way home; I sang Smokey all the way to the altar. And still I sing Smokey every day I'm lucky enough to wake up beside her.

I want to tell the young ones that my daughter is beautiful, with a smile so bright "she could have been a candle." I play Smokey and Curtis for her. I hope many other black fathers of beautiful daughters will play Smokey for their children, too. It will help them understand how they should expect to be treated.

I want to tell the young ones that it will not be easy for anyone to get my daughter away from me. Like her mother, she's a treasure.

And if my daughter's suitors don't know the gospel according to Smokey and Curtis, they won't have any chance at all. I intend to make sure of that.

Whoomp, there it is.

Peggy Peterman

ST. PETERSBURG TIMES

Lest We Forget

Any People who could
endure all that
brutalization and keep
together, who could
undergo such
dismemberment and
resuscitate itself, and
endure until it could
take the initiative in
achieving its own
freedom, is obviously
more than the sum of
its brutalization.
—*Ralph Ellison*

It was always dusk when people began arriving at the brick church on Greenwood Avenue in Tuskegee, Alabama. Those who could walk took their time and strolled down the dusty road to Greenwood Baptist Church, so that they could get a good seat just before the meeting began.

Walking was preferred, because the Alabama nights were fairly cool, in fact, some of the elders wore a light wrap around their shoulders.

Others drove, some came from long distances to the church. It was important to be there, and to be on time.

The Tuskegee Civic Association was sponsoring the meetings, so people knew it was going to be well organized, and it would start on time. Association leaders would take care of business, and then they would leave. That's the way Dr. Charles G. Gomillion, president, and W. P. Mitchell, executive secretary, liked to run things.

People from all walks of life came through the church's double doors. They came to listen to speakers and to gain strength for the remainder of the week—the strength they needed to keep the boycott going. But it wasn't called a boycott, it was called "Trading With Your Friends."

It was 1957, and the Alabama legislature, through a bill sponsored by State Representative Sam Engelhardt, had gerrymandered nearly all of the black people out of the city limits.

But again, they had underestimated black people in this college town. Most white folks in the city and around the state called African-Americans in Tuskegee "uppity Negroes or niggers." It was a town pretty much dominated by middle- and upper-class black people who either worked at the Veterans Administration hospital or for Tuskegee Institute (now Tuskegee University). The people were politically aware, and organized. These mass meetings lasted all through the summer of 1957.

As we waited for the meeting to begin, every once in a while our heads would turn slowly toward the rear to glance at the church door. Seated on the podium, civic association officials glanced expectantly toward the door also. Waiting women gently waved their funeral home fans in front of their faces, and those of their children.

She just had to come tonight.

Then, when we spotted her walking slowly through the door, a joyous murmur started from the back of the church and rippled toward the front, cascading off the pulpit.

After she was seated, we all waited for the slow, deep resonance of her voice. Her aged body rarely moved, as she sang verse after verse.

"Don't you let nobody turn you 'round, turn you 'round, turn you 'round, don't you let nobody turn you 'round . . ."

It was all we needed. Spirits swelled. The elder was singing, we had received our message. Her voice echoed the voices down through the ages. It was the voice of people we'd never seen. It was the voice of old Africans dragged off the boat and onto the plantations. It was the voice of black men and women who endured the slavers' lashes, dirt-floored shanties, childbirth in the fields.

"Don't you let nobody turn you 'round, turn you 'round, ohhh, turn you 'round!"

It was the voice of folks who had sat around a wood-burning stove gently pressing half-empty cups of pot liquor to the lips of infants and children; black people who had walked miles and miles, just to learn how to read and write; men and women who had run away from their bosses, hoping to find a better place to rear their children, and "crazy niggers" who had stood off white nightriders with guns.

They were the voices of those who struggled for freedom, such as Denmark Vessey, Gabriel Prosser, Nat Turner, and Ida B. Wells—and a host of others, who we will never know.

Those voices carried the Tuskegee Civic Association, its NAACP Legal Defense Fund lawyers, and the black citizens of that town to victory at the U.S. Supreme Court, where we won our lawsuit to restore the city's old boundaries in November 1960. In February 1961, the original boundaries were restored. More than half of the white-owned-and-operated businesses downtown were closed. The boycott had been successful.

The voice of that elder is now at rest, but the echo still vibrates in the hearts of all who remember her. Younger citizens of Tuskegee might not know the history of the association and its work, but it still stands as a monument to the strength, dignity, and perseverance of a people who refused to let obstacles stop them.

This same legacy is found in so many towns and hamlets throughout this nation, where people of African descent have struggled, fought, worked, and toiled.

It is a legacy that has been created by our elders, that has been spelled out in tears, unrelenting hard work, brutality, and even death. The legacy was built by black domestics—in Alabama, Georgia, Mississippi, Louisiana, Maryland, Virginia, and other places—who pulled off their aprons, left their mistresses, and lost their jobs just to go vote.

It was created by black farmers who laid down their plows to struggle for freedom, and sometimes lost their lives in doing so. And it was held together by young black adults who wanted to improve the quality of their lives, but instead had to join the ranks of the unemployed after they staged sit-ins, wade-ins, prayed, sang, and marched for freedom around southern court-houses and Confederate squares.

But for sometime now, it is a legacy that seems not to have been heeded, as African-Americans have grappled with unem-ployment, self-destruction, Reaganomics, racism, and the widen-ing divide between the haves and have-nots in this country.

Today, if we look only at the superficial signs of the African-American's existence, we might believe that that strength found in the past has been lost, because the statistics are so overwhelm-ing:

- Some 53 percent of African-American households have sin-gle parents who are in need of day care, health care, and living expenses.
- Because of the hazards, social ills, and homicides experi-enced by African-American males, their life expectancy con-tinues to be among the lowest of all groups in the nation.
- Per capita, the income of African-Americans is approxi-mately 60 percent that of whites.

Asked what happened to the strength and the determination of our forefathers, many African-Americans shrug and say, "Times change." Others say that they don't know what happened, nor do they understand.

Angrily we point to the mercurial rise of neo-Nazi organiza-tions and the young white racist group called skinheads, the burn-ing of the young black stockbroker Christopher Wilson in Tampa, Florida, by two savage young white men, and the attack on black public officials nationwide. We study the glass ceiling, and the lack of black corporate leaders.

And we conclude that indeed W. E. B. Du Bois was correct when he wrote in his book *The Souls of Black Folk:* "The problem of the twentieth century is the problem of the color-line."

Now as we approach the twenty-first century, African-

Americans everywhere are asking, where is the spirit that Du Bois so eloquently wrote about? Where is this weapon we used for so many years against our oppressor? Where is the determination, the ability to strive above and beyond this abyss of racism, and classism, its first cousin? What happened to the song in our hearts, in our throats, and the fire in our eyes? Where is the dignity and self-respect?

Why do some of our children kill themselves and others at the tender ages of 13, 14, and 15, while others sit in their public housing cubicles discussing what kind of coffins they'd like to be buried in? Why can't mothers sit on their porches at dusk in our cities and rock their newborn infants to sleep? Why can't we send a young child to the store without having to worry whether he or she will come home? When did our oppression take its final toll?

There is something much deeper that has happened, and African-Americans must begin to explore the reasons with wisdom— or we won't be able to claim the twenty-first century, which by all rights, should be ours.

There is no way to fight the filthy rise of racism in the workplace, the courthouses, and the schoolhouse, without a foundation—a knowledge of the spirit of our past.

We lost our weapons by losing our African selves, by refusing to continue the great tradition of storytelling, by not explaining to our children where we came from, who brought us here, and how we've overcome so much.

Civil rights activists of the past sit with silent, saddened faces, as black schoolchildren acknowledge that they know nothing about the civil rights movement, and ask, "Who was Martin Luther King, Jr.?"

They know even less about Africa, from which our ancestors came, its civilizations, and the ancient universities, and the Greeks who went there to study and learn from African scholars. Why should we expect our young people to be able to circumvent the physical and psychological traps of this society? We've given them no map, no compass, no guideposts to follow.

We scream and rant at European teachers, demanding that they teach African-American children our history. Then we shake our heads in disbelief, when our children hear only Tarzan stories.

We squander our resources and our hard-earned dollars, often in racist institutions that begrudge our very existence in their corporate structure. We allow plastic surgeons to chisel off our full flat noses and chip away at our beautiful full lips.

We fry and drench our kinky, nappy hair in chemicals that leave us nearly bald and tenderize our brains, while increasing the wealth of the white companies that dominate the haircare market.

We suck in our lips and speak in European tongues at cocktail sips, and poke fun at other African-Americans who don't ape Europeans in their lifestyles and behavior.

Others of us flash Kente cloths, as symbols of unity and African-centered pride during the day, and live European at night. Our children languish in smart private schools, unable to find themselves, and then self-destruct at 16, 20, or 25.

We have lost our African selves, and sold our heritage for a mess of porridge. We have lost the spirit of the elders. The books written by our scholars and Afrocentric literary giants lay gathering dust in our well-stocked libraries, as we sit looking at dysfunctional European families, and African-American buffoons prancing across the television tube and movie screens.

Those who led the way and suffered the indignities of the past cannot rest in peace if we walk into the twenty-first century refusing to carry the mantle they left for us.

Our nights and days must be filled with reading and exploring with our families. We must find ways to connect with those brothers and sisters who cannot find, or see, the way without our help.

We must catch the spirit of the past from those who have refused to let it escape them, such as the black men who have organized into clubs to fight hopelessness, despair, and drug addiction among young black teenagers.

We must recapture the spirit of the past from men and women such as Margaree Valma, a poor grandmother in Clearwater, Florida, who despite hobbling on her second knee implant, cares for her four grandchildren. Every school day, she cooks their breakfasts and sends them off to class.

Sometimes Margaree waits for weeks for her daughter to come home; filthy, unkempt, half-starved, after wandering the streets in search of money from johns—from anyone who can support her drug habit.

But Margaree has never given up. She sings, prays, washes and irons, and writes to politicians, demanding that they recognize the plight of grandparents, black and white, across this nation who are struggling in similar conditions. She's started an organization called Concerned Grandparents. Its members make local appeals for clothing and canned goods to help care for poor children. They baby-sit for one another to relieve the tedium of being housebound.

The spirits of the past are still wandering the face of this nation, searching for more African-Americans who are willing to make such sacrifices. They're waiting, unperturbed by our decades of slumber and neglect. They're waiting for us to recapture the fire of Mary McLeod Bethune, who started a school in a small room in Daytona Beach, Florida, using orange crates for desks, and who lived to see her dream grow into Bethune-Cookman College.

They're waiting for us to capture the spirit of Marcus Garvey, who taught economic independence and unleashed a hunger for our African identity that has not yet diminished.

They're waiting for us to recapture the intellectual fire and determination of Thurgood Marshall and Harold Washington.

They're waiting for the descendants of a mighty civilization to stand flat-footed like civil rights leader Fannie Lou Hamer did in Mississippi, unphased by the obstacles placed in her way, determined to restore the dignity and freedom of her people.

For all of this, they desperately wait.

Dwight Lewis

THE TENNESSEAN

Ed Temple's Tigerbelles

T he Olympic flag that draped
Wilma Rudolph's casket in
November 1994 lies in a rock-
ing chair in the den of Ed Temple's Nashville home.

There are also pictures of Temple and some of his Tennessee
State University women's track team, the Tigerbelles, shown
with Presidents John F. Kennedy, Lyndon B. Johnson, and
Jimmy Carter.

And then there are Olympic medals, trophies, plaques, and
other memorabilia awarded to Temple and members of the wom-
en's track team that Temple coached from 1950 until the spring
of 1994.

The mementos are just a small reminder of one of the greatest
rags-to-riches stories in American history, not just athletics.

"About two weeks ago, somebody sent me a copy of this story
that ran in the *Orange County Register*," Temple said the day he
and I sat reminiscing about the Tigerbelles. "I've since had it
laminated and framed."

The story, written by Miki Turner during Black History
Month in February 1995, was headlined: "Once They Ran the
World." Tennessee State Tigerbelles dominated women's track
meets in the 1950s and 1960s.

"I knew we were great, but when I saw this story from way out in California, I was moved," Temple said.

"Really, for a small, little black school in north Nashville to accomplish what we did was something special," the sixty-seven-year-old Temple said.

Temple is a special person, and his Tigerbelles were simply outstanding.

There were people like Wilma Rudolph, the tall, lanky girl from Clarksville, Tennessee, who had polio and scarlet fever as a child but went on to win three gold medals in the 1960 Olympic Games at Rome.

And there was Edith McGuire, the 5-foot-8-inch speedster from Atlanta who won a gold medal in the 200-meter dash in the 1964 Olympic Games in Tokyo, and a silver medal for finishing second in the 100-meter dash behind fellow Tigerbelle Wyomia Tyus.

Tyus, by the way, became the first woman to win back-to-back gold medals in Olympic competition in the 100 meters when she also finished first in the 1968 Olympic Games at Mexico City.

The list goes on and on. Stars like Mae Faggs, Margaret Mathews, JoAnn Terry, Madeline Manning, Estell Baskerville, Iris Davis, Mamie Rallins, Chandra Cheeseborough, Kathy McMillian, and Brenda Morehead. And there are others.

Ed Temple coached forty Tigerbelles who went on to compete in various Olympic games.

What's more amazing is that thirty-nine of those Tigerbelles graduated from college.

"After Wilma's passing, I have sat in this room and thought a lot about her and the Tigerbelles," Temple said. "Wilma was the glue behind the Tigerbelles. When she traveled, she would visit other Tigerbelles who lived elsewhere around the country. McGuire and Tyus out west, Faggs in the Midwest. She kept them together."

As you listen to Temple talk, you get the feeling that you're about to see the famed Tigerbelles take off running.

"Wilma was the Jesse Owens of women's track and field," Temple said. "She was great."

What really stands out about Ed Temple's Tigerbelles is that they did so much with so little.

"They were the pure of heart," Temple said. "They did it for the sake of accomplishing something and to show that women could do it. They were pioneers.

"We had no Title IX scholarships. They had work-aid. They were glad to get an education. They came out of small towns like Griffin, Georgia, and Clarksville, Tennessee."

Temple credits the late Dr. Walter S. Davis, Tennessee State's second president, with getting the Tigerbelles going.

"He started the program in the late forties," said Temple. "He didn't have to do it, but he did. You have to give him credit. When I came on board as coach after completing college at Tennessee State, Dr. Davis said, 'Take these two station wagons and go where you need to go.'

"We would leave here and go to New York. We would stop for gasoline and we would take brown bag lunches. When we went to the Tuskegee Relays in Alabama, we couldn't stop at service stations and use the rest rooms because of segregation, so we hit the fields.

"Times were tough but everybody enjoyed it. I remember the first time our girls got USA uniforms, it meant something to them. It was a great honor. Now athletes want to know 'How much money will I get?'"

As we sat in his den talking, Temple remembered that when Wilma Rudolph got back from the 1960 Olympic Games, someone wanted to give her a small black and white television set for winning the three gold medals.

"She had to turn it down to make sure she kept her amateur status. It was the times," Temple said. "We were happy to get the opportunity to compete . . . to do what we did. You wanted to be the best. Being from Tennessee State, where the basketball and football teams were winning then, you wanted to win, too.

"We started at the bottom. We didn't win our first national title until 1955. Our first budget was $300, but we started winning and Dr. Davis kept encouraging us. Nobody else had such a great program for women."

Ed Temple and his Tigerbelles are proud people. They have

a right to be. When Temple says his women opened the doors for other females to compete in track and field events, he's telling the truth.

"We had to run against other countries," he said. "TSU carried this country. The Tigerbelles won a total of six gold medals in the 1960 Olympic Games at Rome, and then there was long jumper Ralph Boston from Tennessee State, who also won a gold medal there.

"And we first had an old cinder track here that went around the football field. For our indoor track, we ran through the doors of Kean Hall, our gym," Temple said. "We utilized what we had and went beyond the best. I think we made the whole country proud. Now look at how other schools are trying to follow in our footsteps.

"There have been some great stars from other schools since we first started, but no school has accomplished what the Tigerbelles did. Do you know of any school that had women finish first and second in the 100-meter dash like Wyomia Tyus and Edith McGuire did in the 1964 Olympic Games? Or do you know of any school to send seven women to one Olympic competition like we did in 1960?

"That's saying a lot for the Tigerbelles."

And it's saying a lot for Ed Temple, the man who helped make so many of them Olympic champions.

4

The Color Line—
And Degrees of Blackness

DeWayne Wickham

USA TODAY/GANNETT NEWS SERVICE

The Color Line

The problem of the twentieth century," W. E. B. Du Bois wrote in *The Souls of Black Folk*, his 1903 autobiography, "is the problem of the color-line."

He was right. This has been a century of racial turmoil, a time of unending conflict between America's shrinking white majority, bent on maintaining its race-based privileges, and the nation's restive black minority. Worse, it has been a century in which little of real substance was done to bridge America's great racial divide.

And so it is painfully easy for me to predict that the problem of the twenty-first century, too, will be the problem of the color line.

Race matters in America. It always has. Maybe it always will. There was a brief time in this century when it seemed the gap between blacks and whites was closing. To be sure, it was a small window of opportunity that opened wide sometime around the day in August 1963, when Martin Luther King, Jr., took to the steps of the Lincoln Memorial to give his now famous "I Have a Dream" speech.

But it didn't stay open very long. It started to close on April 4, 1968, when a white assassin's bullet ripped the life from King's body and plunged the nation into a spasm of racial violence. It slammed shut twelve years later when Ronald Reagan was elected president.

In rather short order, America's warm embrace of the general idea of racial equality became a deadly stranglehold as many whites came to see affirmative action as an encroachment upon that to which they feel entitled.

When it comes to the color line, they have a lot more tolerance for evil than good.

The first slave ship docked on these shores in 1619, a year before the *Mayflower* dropped anchor at Plymouth Rock. For the next 246 years slavery was the law of the land. And for 99 years following passage of the Thirteenth Amendment, which abolished slavery, America permitted the practice of a most pernicious form of racial discrimination against its newly freed slaves and their descendants.

Then in 1964, Congress enacted and President Lyndon Johnson signed into law a far-reaching Civil Rights Act, meant to salve the wounds of black America and assuage white America's guilt. The following year—the one hundredth anniversary of the Thirteenth Amendment—Congress passed the Voting Rights Act, opening the way for millions of disenfranchised blacks to exercise this democracy's most important right.

Within weeks of King's murder, Congress acted again. This time by passing a Fair Housing Act that was intended to staunch the rampant discrimination that kept most blacks locked inside urban ghettos or rural squalor.

More than anything else, these new laws caused an explosion in growth of the nation's suburbs as millions of whites fled the cities ahead of an expanding and energized black population that by law could now live, shop, and go to school just about anywhere it chose.

The election of Ronald Reagan in 1980 was an act of white backlash.

By then those whites who had physically or psychologically abandoned the cities were mad enough, and numerous enough, to get even. After less than three decades of efforts to undo the effects of three and a half centuries of slavery and government-sanctioned racial discrimination, they demanded an end to affirmative action programs. They were "tired of being punished," many whites complained, "for the sins of their forefathers"—as if racism and the special advantages it's given white folks is a thing of the past.

But of course it isn't.

It's true the racism of the last years of the twentieth century has taken on a kinder, gentler face. For most of the 1900s it was far more brazen than it is these days.

It was more confrontational.

More in-your-face.

Today's racism is a subtler brand of bigotry. It's wrapped in talk of "reverse discrimination." Disguised in the rhetoric of right-wing conservatives. And hidden just beneath the thin skin of those who say they favor equal opportunity for blacks to gain access to the American mainstream, but not equal results for those of us who work just as hard as they do for the chance.

So for many employers the act of simply considering someone black for a job vacancy meets their equal opportunity test, while calls for them actually to hire qualified blacks is seen by many as an unreasonable demand for equal results.

And there's more.

The blatant housing discrimination of the first half of this century has been replaced in its closing decades by bias in mortgage lending. The current lending bias and redlining practices of banks is just as pernicious and debilitating for today's blacks as the more openly hostile forms of housing discrimination of earlier years. So not surprisingly, the Supreme Court's 1954 decision outlawing racial segregation in public schools has had little real impact.

In the past, public schools were segregated by law. Now they're segregated by white flight and the discriminatory lending practices of mortgage bankers. And to add insult to injury, millions of whites who now send their children to private schools balk at paying higher taxes to support the public systems they deserted. Instead, they press for government programs to help them pay the cost of educating their kids in private schools.

Today racial discrimination in employment is illegal. But the laws that outlaw it have done little to change these realities: 1) black unemployment has been at least double that of whites, in good economic times and bad, for nearly half a century; 2) the jobless rate among blacks with master's degrees is higher than that of whites with just bachelor's degrees; and 3) black college graduates, on average, earn significantly less than their white counterparts.

This much now seems certain, these twentieth-century problems will be with us in the year 2000, and beyond.

In fact, there is mounting evidence that a more virulent form of racist activism has emerged in recent years. Skinheads and the Aryan Nations are the most obvious example. These white supremacist organizations are the linear successors to the Ku Klux Klan. They openly target blacks, Jews, and other minorities for both verbal and physical attacks.

But even more worrisome is the changing political landscape. The closing years of the twentieth century threaten to usher in an end to this nation's second Reconstruction. The first one, which broadly spanned the period from 1865 to 1901—the year the last former slave was ousted from Congress—was a time of dramatic social and political gains for blacks. It ended when Republicans in Congress, more intent upon preserving their political power than on protecting the constitutional rights of former slaves, gave southern states wide latitude to disenfranchise blacks. In short order, blacks—who in the years following the Civil War served in a wide range of state offices and were elected to the Senate and House of Representatives—disappeared from the nation's body politic. The poll tax, grandfather clause, and other Jim Crow laws were used to suppress the black vote. Those who managed to get around these legal obstacles were often violently attacked by klansmen. One way or another, the opponents of the gains made by blacks were determined to take them away. And they did.

For more than half a century following the end of the first Reconstruction, blacks in this country remained largely disenfranchised—both socially and politically.

The second Reconstruction began in the 1960s with the passage of the Civil Rights Act, Voting Rights Act, and Fair Housing

Act. Like the first one, it was a time of great gains for blacks. The number of blacks in Congress grew from just five in the summer of 1964 when the landmark Civil Rights Act became law to forty in November 1992.

During this time, two blacks, Merv Dymally of California and George Brown of Colorado, served as lieutenant governors of their states. L. Douglas Wilder was elected governor of Virginia; blacks in North Carolina and California served as the speaker of their state's legislature; and the number of black mayors and state elected officials increased sharply.

But this progress did not come without great resistance.

Provisions of the Voting Rights Act that brought about the creation of majority-black congressional districts came under fierce attack from those who argued that such gerrymandering was a form of racism that disadvantaged whites. In essence, what they wanted was a return to the days when whites were certain to win election to virtually every seat in Congress—a time when congressional district lines were drawn to keep blacks out of the federal legislature.

The court battles set off by these challenges threaten to sharply reduce the number of blacks in Congress. As a result of the redrawing of congressional district lines following the 1990 census, the number of blacks in the House of Representatives jumped from 27 to 39 following the 1992 election. That same year, Carol Moseley-Braun (D-Ill.), became just the second black to be elected to the Senate in this century. Since its founding in 1970, the Congressional Black Caucus increased in size from 13 to 40 members. Blacks in the 103rd Congress had unprecedented power. Three chaired full committees of the House. Sixteen headed subcommittees in that body.

But those gains proved short-lived. Republicans won control of both houses of Congress in 1994, ousting all Democrats— including those within the black caucus—from their leadership positions. Worst, the new Republican leaders immediately launched a legislative assault on federal spending for programs for the poor. They called for deep cuts in the food stamps and child nutrition programs, plus radical changes in the welfare system.

While the welfare program was long overdue for an overhaul, the changes pushed by the GOP were mean-spirited and unduly harsh. One sought to deny welfare benefits to women under the age of eighteen who have children out of wedlock. Another called for the children of parents kicked off the welfare rolls to be placed in government-run orphanages, a draconian measure that would be far more costly than keeping those women on the Aid to Families with Dependent Children rolls.

These actions came as other attacks were being launched at the state level. In California, a drive was mounted to have residents of the nation's most populous state pass a Constitutional amendment outlawing affirmative action programs.

In Mississippi, state officials sought to end the unnecessary duplication of college programs by closing down most of its historically black higher education institutions, or merging them into predominantly white schools.

State officials in Missouri went before the Supreme Court to argue for an end to federal court oversight of the desegregation of the majority-black public schools in Kansas City. Having been forced by a federal judge to raise taxes to finance more than a billion dollars' worth of improvements to Kansas City's aging and dilapidated school system, state officials objected to the judge's insistence that the schools stay under his control until students' standardized test scores improved.

Many of these attacks were supported by a small group of black conservatives who allied themselves with those who sought to turn back the clock. These quislings are the twentieth-century version of the nineteenth-century's black accommodationists. Some of them mistakenly believe that blacks who press the government and private sector to undertake affirmative action to reverse the effects of racial discrimination seek some special advantage over whites.

Many others, I suspect, are not so naive. They're the Judas goats of the civil rights struggle. One group, called the "Minority Mainstream," publicly embraced the platform of congressional Republicans and called for even tougher measures to roust the poor from their dependence on federal aid. Their complicity in this effort helped shield the real intent of their white handlers.

The black conservative cause was aided in the last decade of the twentieth century by the appointment of Clarence Thomas to the Supreme Court and the election of Gary Franks and J. C. Watts to Congress.

Thomas, a rabid conservative, filled the high court seat vacated by the retirement of Thurgood Marshall. Franks, a Connecticut Republican, was first elected to Congress in 1990. Four years later, Watts won an Oklahoma congressional seat. A one-time star quarterback at the University of Oklahoma, Watts bolted the Democratic party in the late 1980s.

Both Watts and Franks argue that they represent the views of a broad segment of blacks. They're wrong. While many blacks are undeniably conservative on issues like crime and family values, most are wildly liberal when it comes to questions of equal opportunity and affirmative action—the two issues on which Watts and Franks are most stridently conservative.

Not surprisingly, both men represent congressional districts almost totally devoid of blacks. Watts's district is 92 percent white; Franks's is 95 percent white. More revealing is this: not a single black conservative has won election to Congress from a majority-black district this century. That's because their message just doesn't resonate among black voters.

In truth, Watts and Franks are white leaders, not black ones. They represent the interests—and reflect the attitudes—of the white voters who put them in office. Their attempt to portray themselves as black leaders is a thinly veiled sham. Still, Republican conservatives who desperately search for blacks willing to bear their cross, point to Franks, Watts, and Justice Thomas as a new breed of black leaders. Few blacks side with them, but still they persist in making this bogus claim.

All of these things combine to propel our nation into the next century with the race problem of the twentieth century still unsolved.

The possibility is real that the second Reconstruction of blacks will end as abruptly—and with equally menacing results as did the first. If the Supreme Court strikes down the redistricting plans that swelled the numbers of blacks in Congress, our presence in the federal legislature will drop sharply, and with it will fall the faith many blacks have in the American political system.

This loss of faith will be deepened if the Republican-controlled Congress forces its radical social agenda upon the millions of blacks who are stuck at the bottom of the nation's economic system. With little hope of a political rescue, they will become increasingly restive, insular and hostile.

That's a formula for a replay of the racial violence that was with us from start to finish of the twentieth century.

With the new millennium just a few years off, it's a certainty that we won't solve the nation's race problem in this century. But that doesn't mean we are condemned to relive our troubled racial past.

We can do better than we have.

We can accomplish in the next century that which we failed to get done in this one.

We can actually solve our race problem. Of this I am certain. But it'll take more than my wistful belief in a color-blind America for us to overcome our racial hangups.

Somewhere between those radical conservatives who want to rip gaping holes in the nation's social safety net and the far-left liberals who resist any changes in a welfare system that fails to help poor people escape their poverty lies the answer to our racial discord.

Finding it won't be easy. Centuries of racial division and animosities have taken their toll. But if we don't start now to ferret it out we'll doom those who inhabit the next century to relive the racial turmoil of the last.

Lisa Baird

NEW YORK POST

A Churning in
My Gut

The churning started in the stomachs of African-Americans as soon as news spread that four white and Asian suburbanites had been killed by a gunman in a shooting spree aboard a Long Island Rail Road train Tuesday evening.

For some, the initial fluttering was accompanied by a prayer: "Lord, please don't let him be black."

A tragic response, but one many black people experience whenever a horrendous crime is perpetrated, especially against white victims.

It turns out the gunman was indeed black. And with that, the stomach-knotting began in earnest, as African-Americans braced for the inevitable.

"Where are the black leaders? Where is Al Sharpton now? What's Al Sharpton gonna do for me?" asked one shooting victim. His sentiments were echoed by others, including callers who made threats at Sharpton's office.

You see, black people can't just mourn the loss of life or denounce the crime. This society does not allow us that level of humanity. We also have to deal with the fallout, and the double standards and contradictions that fallout reveals.

"The fact that the melanin I share with Colin Ferguson could somehow implicate me in the senseless murders forced me to stop and analyze the current tense racial mood in the New York metropolitan area," says Mack Cauthen.

Cauthen says that since the killings he feels a heightened sense of being watched by white motorists while stuck in traffic on his daily commute to his Long Island job.

"Listening to a certain shock jock on WABC radio continuing to flame the tense racial powder keg certainly does not help alleviate my tension," says the Englewood council president.

He mentions how reports of Ferguson's motive focused on his anger toward whites and Asians, although Ferguson also raged against "Uncle Toms," conservative blacks, black lawyers, and his own black neighbors.

"The fact that Colin Ferguson could have just as easily shot me had I been on that train because I fit the profile of a 'conservative' Uncle Tom seems lost to many in the media," Cauthen says.

He notes the depiction of Ferguson as an "animal."

"Working in Nassau County, I can't recall Joel Rifkin being called an animal, predator, or beast," he says of the (white) accused killer of women, some of them prostitutes.

"Jeffrey Dahmer, whose victims were black and Asian, was not called an animal even though he stored parts of dismembered bodies in a refrigerator. I don't recall Richard Speck, John Wayne Gacy, or David Berkowitz being referred to as animals. I recall these killers being referred to as sick, psychotic madmen."

He says as an afterthought that somehow it must be less tragic when both killer and victims are all white.

And there he has hit on the most blatant double standard demonstrated in the aftermath of the railroad killings.

It is a double standard that makes "black-on-black" crime such a hot topic for cocktail party conversation and presidential sermons in black churches, but not a prompt to any action, unless you consider calling on black America to address its own internal problems taking action.

Day in and day out, black-on-black crime gets discussed—the majority of crime, which is white-on-white, gets cursory attention. And then Colin Ferguson boards a train headed for the kind of bedroom communities where neither kind of crime is supposed to happen, and commits the one crime that gets action: black on white.

The nation is now clamoring for handgun prohibition, death penalties, arming citizens to fight back, you name it. Suddenly, there is consensus that the mindless violence must stop.

Betty Bayé

LOUISVILLE COURIER JOURNAL

Let's Talk Black

J ust say it!

That's what I tell myself when I don my columnist's cap and prepare to take out after some "Negro" who, as my late father would say, has done or said something likely to "set the race back one hundred years."

Growing up with a father who was a race man in the best sense meant always being mindful of how my words and behavior, good or bad, were liable to impact the progress of the race.

So, besides the givens of journalism, I, as an African-American woman and columnist, necessarily find myself having second thoughts about how to tell it like it is about some member of the race when most of my readers are white, including some who make no secret of having an anti-black agenda.

The burden of the African-American columnist working in the majority media is not one shared by our white colleagues, or even by other African-Americans who write in the black-owned media.

In *Ebony, Jet, Essence, Emerge,* or *Black Enterprise,* the African-American can expect to be talking mostly to the people who speak the same language, who can put criticisms into context, and not use them negatively to broad-brush the race.

I contend that the African-American columnist working in the white-owned press is obligated by history to carefully construct his or her words when offering commentary on the touchy subject of race, particularly when anti-black sentiments—and when has that not been so?—run high.

White columnists can criticize bad, ignorant white people all day long because bad white people, no matter how ignorant, no matter how terrible their crimes, still are perceived as individuals.

Bad, ignorant black people, on the other hand, are not perceived as individuals, but as representatives of the race. The irony, of course, is that good black people are generally perceived as individual exceptions to the race.

There are African-American columnists, of course, who don't share my dilemma—one I've heard articulated by other black journalists, columnists and reporters alike. They say they just dish it out, and let the chips fall where they may.

No doubt some African-American columnists are far more cynical in that they've discovered that blacks whose stock and trade is to criticize other blacks are labeled by many whites, liberals among them, as courageous. And so the rewards can be seductive: journalism prizes, book contracts, speaking engagements, and a regular chair on TV with "objective" white colleagues.

Some will argue African-American columnists who have second thoughts about telling it like it is in the white press about errant or deviant members of the race fear that we'll be labeled Uncle Toms.

Who, in their right mind, would relish being labeled a sellout to their people?

Though such thoughts have crossed my mind—I was, after all, black before becoming a columnist—fear of criticism by other blacks or whites is not, in my view, the overriding issue.

I and others like me don't lack courage.

Rather, history dictates for me, at least, that, like my ancestors who worked in the master's house, I must be careful with my words lest they be misunderstood and used for the wrong cause.

As an African-American, history suggests a certain degree of caution given that the race, despite the best efforts of many inside and out of it, remains under siege.

I also must exercise caution when writing on matters of race because black Americans and white Americans often mouth identical words, but the meaning is entirely different.

A columnist should add to the dialogue, not to the confusion.

As an African-American, no matter my education and profession, I bear the legacy of slavery, of Jim Crow, of lynchings, of segregation, of white media that have sometimes deliberately and sometimes inadvertently advanced an anti-black agenda.

Whenever I push this dark brown face into places where such a face has never been, I'm not merely a journalist, but an emissary of those who've long been unable to explain their version of events.

So, for reasons of color, history, and whose daughter I am, in my deeds and actions I was never not conscious of the possible consequences for THE RACE.

As an African-American columnist I put words on paper about us with the knowledge that I'm liable to be damned if I do, and damned if I don't, but will be more damned if I'm not principled about whatever position I argue.

Racism, whether one is a college-educated opinion writer, a corporate executive, or the one with the meanest, lowest-paying job, requires victims to be ever mindful of its existence. Racism requires us, I contend, always to be careful and conscious of what we say, how we say it, and when and where we say it.

It's not about African-American columnists being afraid or unwilling to write negatively about African-Americans who deserve to be exposed.

It's about the reality that a substantial percentage of what passes for truth on matters of race in America is not truth, but white perceptions. The truth about race in America is, in fact, difficult to uncover since it is colored by history and race.

The African-American columnist knows this, and, in many instances, we've grown up aware that white perceptions masquerading as truths are what have and continue to make life for many of us hell.

Michael Paul Williams

RICHMOND TIMES-DISPATCH

What's in a Name?

I told you be true to the
game. Write something
with backbone, black
man. Don't be a sellout
your whole life.

    **P.S. Stop!!! calling
yourself and others
African-Americans. We
are all African.**

I'd like to know why
blacks are calling
themselves
African-Americans.
Anyone who hyphenates
their name is
un-American, as if
they're Africans first
and Americans second.
—Anonymous letters

Behold the ugly African-American.

    Years after the term's introduction into our vernacular, U.S. citizens of African descent still are in disagreement over what we should call ourselves.

    It's not surprising that "African-American" has been met with anger and stiff resistance by whites, who view it as threatening, militant, or unpatriotic.

But even black Americans are far from unanimous over the term, which begs the question: How can we figure out where we're going if we can't decide who we are?

A survey by the Roper Organization of New York shows only 30 percent of blacks in the United States prefer the term "African-American." Forty-two percent prefer "black"; 10 percent prefer "Afro-American"; and 18 percent prefer some other term, or don't know.

The survey also showed blacks—we'll use the most popular term here—split along generational lines. Most young blacks choose "African-American" while most older blacks prefer "black."

This isn't the first time, of course, that we've been engaged in a controversy over what to call ourselves.

As a youngster growing up during the "revolution"—which, despite Gil Scott-Heron's claim to the contrary, was indeed televised from Watts, Newark, and Detroit—I watched a Bill Cosby–hosted TV series create snapshots of the state of black America during the late sixties.

My most vivid recollection of that series was a segment in which little kids were asked who they were—colored, Negro, black, Afro-American? The confusion and pain on some of their faces made the exercise seem like an act of cruelty.

But it didn't take much longer than a James Brown shout before most of us were black and proud. "Negro" and "colored" became, for the most part, quaint terms relegated to history books, old newspapers, magazines, and the unyielding vocabulary of our elders.

Good riddance. Even as a child, the word *Negro* wounded me. Maybe it was the close resemblance to the other N-word—and lazy southern diction that transformed Negroes into "Nigras." But even when pronounced properly, the word sounded too damned anthropological, conjuring unflattering Darwinian images. If we were Negroes, why weren't whites calling themselves Caucasians?

Colored was more soothing to the ear—we were, after all, people of color. But the word was so ambiguous, considering the many hues within the race, and outside. If we were colored, I wondered, what did that make people in China? And India? And Brazil? And what of the Indians?

So it became a black thing—and I guess I understand. In the shorthand we find it necessary to function in in a sound-bite world, black is concise and the appropriately sharp counterpoint to white—even if the folks who call themselves black come in hues ranging from charcoal to chocolate, from café au lait to cream.

"Black is a state of mind," a cinnamon-skinned sister once told me.

A state of mind apparently unshared by many people of color with Hispanic surnames, or some brothers and sisters who hail from the Caribbean. They may look like us, but their histories and experiences differ in texture and tone. At times, I suspect, they don't much understand us or the "black thing."

But are we really Africans, as the brother who accused me of being a "sellout" forcefully asserts?

Even the executive secretary of a mainstream organization like the Virginia State Conference has taken to referring to us as "Africans."

But I don't think so.

As I conversed with brothers from Senegal during a trade conference between southern governors and African heads of state, I couldn't help but be struck by the chasm that separated us.

Even as I proudly walk the streets wearing Kente cloth, I must admit that many of us have shamefully romanticized Africa while being blind to its problems. Beyond our ignorance, what separates us from Africa is four hundred years of struggle that has shaped us, for better or for worse, into what we are today. A people who've overcome tremendous adversity. A nation within a nation, some of us rising to dizzying heights, others mired in dismal conditions, others maintaining or struggling between the extremes.

A people whose unpaid labors and against-the-odds achievement built a nation.

Nothing has mocked this nation's hypocrisy more than our ability to overcome. By weaving dreams from a nightmare, African-Americans—more than any other group—represent the true American ideal.

To cast that aside would be a slap in the face of our ancestors. To call ourselves Africans, without the hyphen, is an admission of defeat rather than a display of conceit.

But to call ourselves African-Americans makes perfect sense to me.

After years of being told who we were—colored, Negro, nigger—"black" became an assertion of self-determination. African-American takes that a step further. It's an acknowledgment of heritage, of roots. With self-awareness comes empowerment. I suspect that's what threatens some folks.

This homage to the motherland is something that Europeans —Italian-Americans, Irish-Americans, Polish-Americans, and others—have exercised without having their patriotism questioned. Why has it become an issue when black people joined in?

For anyone to question the relative patriotism of African-Americans—who've died in disproportionate numbers in defense of a country that continues to waffle at the idea of guaranteeing us our full rights as citizens—borders on the obscene.

So the struggle continues, with more joint cooperation between us and our brothers and sisters across the Atlantic. Summits between Africans and African-Americans, seeking ways to improve the lot of both our peoples, solidify the long-lost ties between us.

So there you have it. African-American is my preference.

Even so, "black" will always have a special place in my heart because of its undeniable link to our resurgent pride.

Brenda Payton

OAKLAND TRIBUNE

Black Like Me

Some years ago, a dark-skinned woman friend of mine let me in on one of her private rituals. Whenever she enters a social gathering of African-Americans, a reception, a party, or a lecture, she automatically calculates the number of light-skinned versus dark-skinned people in attendance.

Click click, this is a light-skinned set.

Click click, this one is a dark-skinned gathering.

I thought it was a strange obsession. The next time I went to an African-American party, I tried her calculation, to prove she was unreasonably obsessed with color. I didn't. Only one person in the room was darker than light brown, and she had just returned from Jamaica. I repeated the ritual at the next party and observed the same hue. At a museum reception I stepped back from the crowded room to get an overall sense of the shade—it was light.

In a good number of the gatherings I've since observed, the crowd is mostly either light or dark, with a few medium browns and one or two tokens of the "opposite" hue.

My friend was correct. We continue to practice intra-group segregation along color lines.

It wasn't the first time I had noticed that groups of African-Americans are often either light or dark. I attended an elite, mostly white private college during the early 1970s. The black students were privileged and bright, but also down with the cause. We organized several community programs, including a freedom school in the black community and an education program for the brothers at the nearby state penitentiary. During the first class meeting in the prison, I was struck by the color contrast. The college students, on one side of the tables, were light; the prisoners, on the other side of the tables, were dark. An hour earlier I would've described the college students as a group of mixed browns. But compared to the brothers in the penitentiary we didn't look mixed brown at all; we were light.

Recently a woman friend was doing some work in a California prison and commented on how handsome the brothers are inside. And she noticed something else. As a group, they were unusually dark—darker than the average group of dark-skinned African-Americans. Her observation didn't constitute a study, but it made us wonder whether the prisoners had been programmed to fail by teachers, relatives, a society that expected them to be trouble-makers or stupid because they were exceptionally dark.

In 1991, two sociologists, Veran Keith and Cedric Herring, documented the correlation between status and skin color. They found dark-skinned African-Americans had lower income and lesser status in the black community. The previous year, sociologists Michael Hughes and Bradley Hertel found similar disparities based on skin color. Even when they adjusted for the fact that light-skinned African-Americans are more likely to come from wealthier families, the researchers found that light-skinned African-Americans had better education and occupation opportunities. Further, the income gap between light-skinned and dark-skinned people was comparable to the income gap between African-Americans and white Americans; dark-skinned African-Americans made 72 cents for every $1 earned by light-skinned African-Americans.

The fact is, and we all know it, in almost every aspect of life —education, career, romance, beauty, income—opportunity is determined by skin color. (The exceptions are appropriately in the fields of jazz and blues, where African-Americans created and defined the forms in a context that was more removed from the values of the white-dominated society.)

Within the group, being light-skinned is even more of an advantage than being white in the general society.

That reality is the best-kept secret everyone knows. We are all aware of the tensions, distrust, disparities, divisions between us along color lines, but we all claim that we're not the ones who are color-struck. There are traces of the theme running through our literature, Wallace Thurman's *The Blacker the Berry*, and Spike Lee's *School Daze*, but they are mere traces. We have the sense this is a topic we've heard about ad nauseam, but the discussion is almost always superficial and fleeting.

There has been little academic study of this issue. As I was researching this piece, I called several African-American psychologists who said no, they weren't studying this issue and they didn't know anyone who is, before adding, "Maybe we should take a look at it."

The Color Complex: The Politics of Skin Color Among African-Americans, by Kathy Russell, Midge Wilson, and Ronald Hall, published in 1992, is the first book to address this topic head-on.

We make reference to each other's color in graphic detail— chocolate brown, cinnamon brown, paper bag brown, high yellow, red bone, blue black, meringue, jet black, café au lait—and yet we claim it doesn't matter.

We sound just like white people when confronted with their racism. And maybe it's the same issue. Maybe our being color-struck is just an internalized offshoot of white racism.

I'm not sure.

There's no question it originated in slavery, based on black subjugation and white supremacy. Its antecedents were raw practicality. A light child was related to the master of his race. In the darkest center of slavery, that might have been the best future a mother could give her child—a light skin meant a position in the house, a pair of shoes, whatever slight consideration the father might show his child even as he kept him or her as his chattel.

(And what a bizarre concept—a man could sire a being that was subhuman. What did that reveal about the white masters' sense of their own humanity?)

Just as it does today, lighter skin translated into better opportunity. And it didn't take long for the cycle to be repeated and the conclusion self-perpetuated. The black people who were educated, who got better jobs, were light. Just look at old copies of the Howard University yearbook. (My father, who is light by anyone else's standard, was turned away from an African-American medical school in the 1940s because he wasn't light enough.) If light skin was originally valued because it was a step closer to white, it now has its own value within the African-American community, independent of a white standard. Light skin became indelibly linked to success, supremacy within the race, and beauty.

Beauty. The saga of light-skin beauty requires its own history and analysis. The woman who could ensure the light skin of a man's children was the most desirable, or if she could lighten up the progeny, all the better. Just as blonds define beauty in the general society, light skins with straight hair define it within the African-American community. It's become our own standard of beauty, independent of the white standard; we've all known brothers who genuinely don't find white women attractive but exclusively date light-skinned black women. Try another social calculation as an experiment—note the complexion of the wives of powerful, famous, and rich African-American males, and make a tally of how many are light-skinned and how many could even be classified as medium brown.

Which is not to say that dark-skinned African-Americans have accepted the discrimination without a fight. They, like African-Americans in the larger society, form protected groups where they aren't subjected to the colorism of the light skins. And in a lot of cases, light skins aren't generally welcome, unless they first prove they don't subscribe to color supremacy.

A thirty-two-year-old woman who described herself as light said she works hard to make contact with dark-skinned women. "After I've broken the ice, they'll say, 'Oh, when I first saw you,

I thought you were stuck up.' I say, 'But why did you think that? I never said or did anything.' "

The dark skins don't trust the light skins and the light skins turn around and say they resent the attitudes of the dark skins who assume they will be stuck up and uppity because of the shade of their skin. Man, what a mess.

Of course there are exceptions, African-Americans who are truly color-blind, who somehow escaped the color complex as they were growing up. People whose complexions fall in the middle, neither dark nor light, may be the least affected by the divisions.

But until we take a thorough, hard, unflinching look at this problem, we can never hope to heal the wounds of slavery and achieve racial unity. And once we finally take it on, we shouldn't expect to solve it overnight. It took nearly four hundred years to create; it's going to take a lot of time, honesty, hard work—and determination—to undo.

To Be Young, Gifted, and . . .

Brenda Payton

L et's see, now we're African-Americans. Although I understand that some people have already shortened the term to Afro-American, which was of course one of the names we tried back in the 1960s. If any of us could remember that long ago, we might consider it ironic, or cyclical or something.

I also understand that the most conscious of the young conscious crowd are referring to us as Africans. No hyphenated or double name for them. They are Africans, pure and simple. I remember making a statement something like that a few decades back. That was before I lived in West Africa and discovered it is impossible to be "an African" if you don't even know your ethnic group, also known as your tribe.

But if the most conscious of the young conscious crowd want to be Africans in absentia, it probably won't hurt anything. We have become the masters of multi-labeling. We can be a group of Africans, Afro-Americans, African-Americans, and, for the slow-to-change, black people. We all know what we mean, don't we?

Although I must say, the process of changing our group name has escalated. It used to be that every thirty years or so we would turn on the name we had been using for the previous thirty years and reject it as Uncle Tom lackeyism. Colored became Negro, and then Negro became black. The change is always instant and uncompromising.

We might have been Negroes on Monday, but on Wednesday we were black. Anyone who used the word Negro on Thursday was branded an Uncle Tom lackey unless he or she was using it to label someone else an Uncle Tom lackey. Back in 1968, the phrase "those Negro leaders" didn't need adjectives such as "handkerchief-head"; the exaggerated pronunciation of "N-e-e-g-r-o" said it all. Do you think other groups of people are as hard on themselves as we are? You have to toe the line to be African-American; there's not much room for deviation.

These take-no-prisoners name changes are somewhat trying for anyone over forty who has spent any length of time using the previously acceptable but newly despised term. Recently I was reminded of my parents' difficulties with the Negro-black changeover when I slipped and used the word *black* while talking to a group of the young conscious who could not conceal their disdain. One of them even corrected me. "African-American please, sister."

I wondered if I had ever been so rude and audacious. And realizing that of course I had, I wondered if my parents had suppressed the urge I was suppressing to scream: "Have you lost your mind, you little whippersnapper? Don't you know I was organizing, marching, reading black poetry, being militant, and blacker-than-thou before your parents even knew each other's names? Don't you realize I was the first one in my crowd to read *Wretched of the Earth?* You don't have a clue about the struggles we endured. The tear gas, the police attacks. Don't lecture me about black consciousness or whatever the latest, more African-American-than-thou term you little upstarts want to use." My parents might have phrased it somewhat differently, but their sentiment would probably have been the same.

Now our group name changes occur at shorter intervals. It is almost happening simultaneously. The change from black to African-American had not even penetrated through to those of us who raised holy hell to change the name from Negro to black, when we started hearing offshoots of Afro-American and African. Anyway, we all know what we mean, don't we?

An aside: Thank goodness for the change from black. I'm still breaking the habit of using the term, but for me the switch is long overdue. It sounded great when James Brown shouted, "Say it loud, I'm black and I'm proud." But it was problematic, particularly for those of us who write for a living. If you worked for "the white man's" press, the stylebooks prohibited the capitalization of black. You might write Black children/women/men until you were blue in the face, but the next morning it would always read black children/women/men in the newspaper. We were stuck with a proper noun that wasn't capitalized. In a list of people with color—Asians, Latinos, American Indians, there we were, little-b blacks. We were typographically inferior. Further, it was grammatically incorrect, which is even more damaging than being politically incorrect. Black is an adjective, not a noun. That misuse led to dehumanizing phrases such as "Blacks protest weakening of Voting Rights Act." What exactly are blacks, and why do they care about the Voting Rights Act?

When we were black, I was tempted to return to the term Negro, largely because it was capitalized. A group of my friends threatened to run me out of town on a rail if I did. So I didn't. But I tried to recall why we despised Negroes so intensely. And I couldn't.

Anyway. Today the process, let's call it the art, of continual name change takes on new and challenging complexity. Perhaps the changes will actually happen simultaneously. As soon as the new name is spoken, the next new name will be identified as the truer, most righteous, preferred usage. We will have added name fluidity to our many innovations and creations with language, music, and movement. As Michael Jordan redefined the concept of gravity and Thelonious Monk, space, we will redefine the very concept of label, challenging the presumption of a single label.

Why not have a continually changing, multi-labeled name? It would symbolize our true status as a group—dynamic, mixed, complex. Imagine how interesting it will be when we begin to incorporate the other racial strains in our group bloodline. We can be African-American Indian Americans, which could easily be shortened to Indian African-Americans. And for those bold (or brainwashed, depending on your point of view) enough to acknowledge the European strain, there's another range of possibilities. European Indian African-Americans. Or Indo Euro Afro Amos. That's just the tip of the iceberg.

So name change, even continual and simultaneous name change, doesn't bother me. As awkward as it might feel—you are just about to say "black"—your mouth opening wide on the "bla" when you catch yourself and quickly close your lips around the "af" sound and you end up saying something incoherent like "Blafrican Americans"—even in those uncomfortable moments, the dynamism of continual name change is stimulating. Imagine how boring it would be if we woke up day after day, year after year, decade after decade, always knowing the name for our racial classification. That doesn't even sound like us. Besides, whatever term or terms we use, we all know what we mean, don't we?

Jeff Rivers

HARTFORD COURANT

White Christmases,
Black Santas

Santa Claus is white. No getting around that. My father tried. And I've tried. But facts are facts. Santa Claus is white. White as Rhett Butler.

In the late 1950s, my father tried to get around Santa Claus being white by ignoring the original jolly old elf. He viewed Santa as a silly notion that should be shaken from black children's heads, the way Rhett wanted thoughts of Ashley Wilkes shaken from Scarlett O'Hara's head in *Gone With the Wind*. Daddy didn't want me to think that "some white man in a red suit" gave me the things my parents worked so hard to provide. He didn't want me to think that a white man was likely to give me anything but grief.

Consequently, he was relieved when I, in my five-year-old wisdom, told him I never believed in Santa Claus. The fireplace in my house was sealed. Santa, white or otherwise, had no way to get in, I said.

Years passed and the son became the father. During my daughter's first Christmas in 1988, my wife and I looked all over Oakland until we found a black Santa. We were miffed that we had to go through so much trouble to find one. After all, Oakland was dominated by people of color.

Nevertheless, most of the Santas in that chocolate- and rainbow-swirl city were white.

We had two pictures that year, one with a white Santa and one with a black reindeer-meister. The white Santa was better-looking; his beard was more real. His belly seemed more real, too.

But my wife and I thought the black Santa would be better for our little girl. We didn't want her to grow up, as we had, with her childhood wonderland populated solely by white images, from fairy princesses to the Easter Bunny to Santa Claus.

My wife and I sought to live the vision outlined in Marie Evan's poem "Vive Noir": "i'm gonna put black angels in all the books and a black Christ-child in Mary's arms./i'm gonna make black bunnies black fairies black santas . . ."

After all, I thought, Santa's a classical cultural icon. As such everyone has a right to Santa, everyone can portray him in their own image. It was time to open up Santa to some color-blind casting. Not only was it time for black Santas, but it was time for Latino Santas, Asian Santas. Whatever.

And I still think so. But I also think that it's time to accept that Santa is as European as Cleopatra is African.

For me, accepting the European basis of Santa Claus and enjoying him anyway is another step in truly embracing multiculturalism. Santa Claus is, like jazz, a magical part of American culture.

For too long, white America could only accept black cultural innovations if they could be represented in white face. In some ways, my insistence that the secular spirit of Christmas be represented by a black Santa was no better than white folks presenting Paul Whiteman as the "King of Jazz," Elvis as the "King of Rock," or Vanilla Ice as the "King of Rap."

So while black love and black music will always be the most important part of my not-so-white Christmases, white Santa Clauses will be as welcome in my house as Nat King Cole singing "The Christmas Song."

Even if I don't have a chimney.

"Joy Spring"

Jeff Rivers

f the two white men had just kept on their way, I would have brushed aside being called a nigger by one of them, as if it were soot that had fallen on me from another time. Brushed it aside, the way I and millions of other black men brush aside daily attacks, great and small, on our humanity. Brush them aside to keep a job. Brush them aside to stay out of jail. Brush them aside to stay sane.

But the two men in the pickup truck didn't keep going. They stopped and parked their truck no more than two blocks from me, as if they didn't know or care that their insult, compounded by their nonchalance, caused me to consider beating them to death.

They got out of the truck. Midday midtown traffic hurried on, as the men should have. They talked casually to each other. They didn't have a care in the world. They were not afraid. They didn't have sense enough to know that this time, this one time, the fear that too many white Americans have of black men would have been well founded.

They didn't see me watching them. They didn't feel me debate over whether it would be better to hit one and then the other or just bash the two men's heads together for starters.

Fresh-faced, the sun highlighting the red tints of their skin, especially on their necks, wearing painters' hats and smiles, they looked as if they were part of a chorus in a Gene Kelly musical. They were not big. They did not seem to be armed. They were not afraid. But they should have been.

Just ninety seconds before, the one I had decided to hit called to me from the driver's side of the truck. His voice reminded me of the billboards hawking malt liquor or menthol cigarettes in poor black neighborhoods: it was a seductive mask stretched over an obvious contempt for me.

"Sir," he began, "would you like to buy some speakers?" I ignored him, just as I wish more young black men would ignore the malt liquor billboards.

He then removed his mask. "I thought you might want to buy some speakers for your house, seeing as how you are a nigger."

Ten years had passed since the last white person called me a nigger.

I remember walking across the campus of a small midwestern liberal arts college where I taught high school students the basics of journalism. I moved to the beat of a different drummer. It was Max Roach keeping time as Clifford Brown rang out "Joy Spring." I hummed along. I was on my way to the center of town to get a 95-cent slice of blueberry pie. After I ate my pie, I planned to watch the boys play baseball on the town's field of dreams while I read the newspapers from the big cities, which seemed so far away. I didn't have a care in the world.

"Niggar!"

It was as if someone had reached out and smacked me in the face.

Without thinking, I ran two steps toward the voice. It came from a car that was speeding away. There were six college-aged white men in the car. Though I haven't had a fight since 1969—and I lost—and despite being just five-foot-six and 128 pounds, I have always felt they were lucky to have been moving so fast. Righteous anger is a powerful voice.

Ten years passed.

Through the years, taxicab drivers have refused to pick me up. Store clerks followed me. Bosses have praised comments from white colleagues that I made months before without notice. The Willie Horton ads helped George Bush get elected. Rodney King was beaten. The police who beat King were acquitted in their first trial. Men and women of all races have stepped faster or crossed the street to avoid me. All those actions and many more have shouted nigger at me.

And I brushed them all off.

But this was different. This was two white men, one calling me a nigger in broad daylight and neither of them having a care in the world.

This was the way it used to be for black folks, everywhere, all the time. Disrespect without consideration or fear of consequence. It was as if being called a nigger by these men transported me back to the Georgia my grandfather fled seventy years ago. Moreover, being called a nigger by these men made me consider that my grandfather's Georgia and my Hartford weren't as different as they should be, as I wanted them to be for my son and daughter. That's what angered me so.

The men had been having fun with me. And when the fun was over, I could be dismissed with a word. Nigger.

After a while, I smiled. Then my smile became a knowing laugh. It's a laugh that black men use when they know that they either have to laugh or commit murder.

I turned away from the men and started down the street. I wanted to summon Clifford Brown to play "Joy Spring." But the song wouldn't stay in my head.

"Joy Spring" is for those who feel as if they don't have a care in the world.

Deborah Mathis

GANNETT NEWS SERVICE

Ghettocentrism

We met over a lively debate about the status of American Blackness, specifically the search for our African roots and its current touchstones: Kente cloths, braided hair, and the coinage of the term "African-American."

"You black people in America aren't Africans," my Nigerian friend insisted. "Your ancestors were African, but not you. Most of you don't even know where in Africa your ancestors are from. Many of you can't even locate an African nation on the map. Some of you don't even know where Africa is."

My initial reaction was to take umbrage at the man's apparent determination to distance himself from me, as the moment's representative of black America. Indeed, I had expected a different reception from this, my brother, fresh from the motherland where, I presumed, at least my soul belonged whether or not my feet ever touched its soil.

How dare he talk to me in that superior tone, tinged with taunting amusement. How dare he ridicule so earnest an effort to connect with the beginning, to ferret our heritage, to embrace the roots of our very existence. Shouldn't this evoke from native

Africans, if not wholehearted endorsement, at least halfhearted sympathy? Weren't we all, somehow, family?

Cousins maybe, he would have me know. Distant cousins. Related, possibly, by some long ago diluted bloodline and no doubt united by the eternal quest for equal regard, yet different.

Unlike Africans, American blacks, he noted, have two obstacles: white prejudice against black people and black prejudice against blacks.

"Before we can embrace you as our brothers and sisters," he said, "you have to make yourself whole."

Now, I doubt that all Nigerians, Ghanians, Kenyans, Sengaleses, etc., are in spiritual lockstep. In fact, what little I do know about the various African societies is enough to assure me that I'm correct in thinking my friend and his fellow continentals have some healing of their own to do—witness Angola, Somalia, and Ethiopia—but his own point is considerable.

No conscientious—or conscious—black American can deny the fracture among us. In spots, the separations are gaping, oozing, and sore.

Intraracial factionalism turns on many familiar fronts: economic status, education, religion, region, political affiliation, and hues of skin. Not that it makes us any different from any other human group. It's just that in our case, it makes less sense and, arguably, does more damage, since our continuing march toward justice requires unanimity—pushing in one direction, rather than pulling, internally, at the parts.

Of course, the prejudices we use to size up one another are often based on misguided perceptions and, occasionally, naked envy.

Middle- and upper-class blacks, once considered the backbone and torchbearers of black industry, may be nowadays dismissed as sellouts, begrudged for their good living rather than admired for their hard work, as if not being poor rebukes not only poverty but the impoverished.

Some years ago, I joined a program sponsored by a women's rights organization that proposed dispatching teams of women from all walks of life into a particularly troubled public housing project. As our ranks included everyone from seamstresses to custodial workers to educators, lawyers, doctors, and journalists, our plan was to provide whatever services were needed. We would clean houses, tutor children, make curtains, prepare meals, run errands, bandage knees and elbows, write letters, provide legal counseling. Whatever. Gratis.

The intention—obviously, I would think—was to help people who, for whatever reasons, needed it. Nothing other than satisfaction would accrue to any of the project workers.

"I just have one piece of advice," said one woman who happened to live in the housing project we had targeted. "Don't come driving up in your Jaguars and Mercedes-Benzes."

Of the fifteen women assembled for the project, perhaps one owned a Jaguar or Mercedes-Benz. Most of us were of moderate means; some were downright poor. Not one of us had hit the lottery or inherited a fortune. Anything we had, we had earned the hard way.

The dissenter's logic was, as suspected, lame. The intended beneficiaries would not trust black folks driving up in cars about which they hardly dared even to dream, she said.

Yet she conceded that what everyone wants is, if not the fancy car itself, then at least the reasonable possibility of owning one, the means with which to own it if one so chose. It is, after all, the dope dealer's chief appeal—not the treachery of his trade, but the sizable income he derives from it and the privilege of spending it willfully.

Notably, Jaguar-owning dope dealers are not prohibited from driving through. But the two-faced standard has a crueler irony. It forgives white people who may circumvent housing projects altogether in Rolls-Royces while holding black people to a provincial standard of a kind of ghettocentrism, which maintains, "Either you're with us or you're not. And if you're with us, you must live like us." Unfortunately, this is what passes, these days, for black solidarity.

So, too, are educational parameters used to determine black legitimacy. Educated blacks may be derided as "trying to be white" or criticized for "trying to sound white" or "talking proper." This, too, flies in the face of the competence that blacks have long rightfully claimed.

Use the command of language for the militant rantings and you're a hero. Use it, however, in casual conversation and one runs the great risk of being pegged as "high society."

Religious differences make for a less significant rift, but memorable arguments have been waged over black adherence to Catholicism, Episcopalianism, and mythical faiths, which may be seen as a break with heritage or tradition. In other words, under this warped value system, some religions and denominations are blacker than others.

Then there's the regional thing. I am often taken aback by northern, eastern, and western black Americans who, in all probability, are no more than a generation or two removed from the southern quadrant, but who do not hesitate in sniffing at those of us who are born and reared in the South and choose to stay.

By their estimation, the decision indicates a slave mentality, whereby southern blacks—accustomed to life among born-again rednecks—are afraid to venture far from the plantation setting, lest we be burdened with more freedom than we can manage. To hear them tell it, black enterprise and progress in Mississippi, Alabama, Georgia, Arkansas, Texas, and Louisiana are oxymoronic, unable to coexist except as figments of black imagination and white legerdemain.

Politics? Lord have mercy.

Where white America has latched on to the notion that all blacks are created Democrats and vote that way, black America has publicly repudiated the idea, but privately trains a skeptical eye on nonconformists.

We do not suffer black Republicans gladly, nor black Libertarians to any great extent, but these disagreements are the cosmetics of the issue. It is unfortunate that the main measuring stick for the so-called black voter monolith is political party affiliation when it is so inaccurate a gauge.

A raft of modern surveys and studies shows that significant numbers of black voters hold conservative ideas on a variety of matters. Of course, conservatism is, like liberalism, subjective and relative, which must be considered in reading the surveys. Nonetheless, conservative organizations like the Republican party have seized upon the reports and have lured black members on the promise that they will see action—politically, socially, and economically.

In all probability, what these surveys have unearthed is, generally speaking, black America's respect for and love of tradition, which is kin to, but not the twin of conservatism, at least not as defined in the current partisan realm.

Heretofore, the champions of our best interests—including the traditions we revere—were cloistered in the Democratic party. Since FDR, the Democratic party has been the one linked to the civil rights and social services we collectively deserved and craved.

This is not to say that while we were at the vanguard of these liberal programs we were either all liberals or all conservatives. We were always a mixture, which is why the black monolith is mythical—no more than a surface creature with nothing below.

Even while saying this, however, I remain leery of black Republicans because I have yet to find the GOP's appeal. Identifying oneself as a black conservative is one thing; to pledge oneself to the Republican party—when it has yet to prove worthy of such a commitment—is another. At the same time, I support the divide-and-conquer approach of such diverse allegiances—intellectually, that is. My heart is still wrestling with it.

Finally, the skin game—the literal color of the skin—remains a popular pastime both within black America and without. Fair-complexioned blacks are often assumed to think themselves somehow better than their darker brothers and sisters and, in a throwback to slavery, are believed to be the preferred stock of whites.

The latter presumption may well be true for all I know, which isn't much since I have never broached the subject with white folks and have never gotten inside one's head. But that's beside the point.

If fair-skinned black Americans are traveling about with a sense of superiority, the joke's on them, I'm afraid. In a country that once codified ethnicity based on fractional parentage, to assume that a light complexion is a determinant of any essential thing is a fool's game. They and any darker-skinned disbelievers can rest assured, when the crap gets dished, a mere drop of black blood proves magnetic.

All of these fractures amount to a seriously injured black society hobbling, on crippled limbs, not forward but in circles.

Some of those who have worked hard and studied and achieved have either withdrawn from their ethnic roots and melted down into the larger society to the extent that they are more mush than mettle, or they behave with great apology and curse their own accomplishments. Hence, the selection of African textiles, hairdos, and traditions does not always bespeak a pride in one's blackness, but sometimes a shame in one's Americanism. Likewise, talking "street," remaining in the " 'hood," driving a "hoopty," and "hangin' with the Baptists" are not necessarily testaments to one's down-to-earthness, but may be signal guilt over having options that others do not.

Some have even questioned their own "authenticity," apparently believing that social status, education, and assimilation have immunized them against racism, or at least its most heinous touch. In fact, the so-called black experience is not singular or one-dimensional but capable of many forms. We do not live, think, or thrive the same way, or on the same things. Yet, none are spared racial discrimination. Somehow, it always finds us, rendering the "search for authenticity" an absurdity. Every black experience is the real thing.

It is important that the distinction be drawn among black pride, which celebrates black achievement, competence, and self-sufficiency; Afrocentrism, which rejects white ideas and ideals in deference to the African legacy; and blacker-than-thouism, which supposes that genuine blackness can be mortgaged, worn on the sleeve, or tripped off the tongue.

What I took from my Nigerian friend's admonition was that the first of these options—black pride—is the appropriate exercise if the objective is reunification.

Black America must heal itself, notwithstanding government programs and public policy. It begins with the rejection of blacker-than-thouism, which creates a contest among black people, qualifying participants on the basis of new, self-imposed ste-reotypes.

Unfortunately, disciples of this trend have been emboldened by a raft of writings and speeches by otherwise worthy black Americans who engage in this roundup, possibly to assuage their own sense of lost identity.

Decades ago, a French essayist wrote a book about what happens when intellectuals, exploiting a popular rage, collaborate with people to collect, organize, and grow their wrath, rather than to dissolve it. In *La Trahison des Clercs* (The Treason of the Intellectuals), Julien Benda wrote:

> *Thanks to the progress of communication and, still more, to the group spirit, it is clear that the holders of the same political hatred now form a compact, impassioned mass, every individual of which feels himself in touch with the infinite numbers of others, whereas a century ago such people were comparatively out of touch with each other and hatred in a "scattered" way.*

Benda condemned European intellectuals who abandoned their universal duty to objectivity and, instead, leased their logic to particular factions who craved accreditation and license for devilish designs.

The book is, in fact, esteemed for pinpointing the ideas and emotions that put France and Germany on the road to World War II.

A world war may not be riding on the intolerance of intraracial diversity. But tragedy certainly is. The expanding canyon separating one black American from another is already so wide and deep in some places that in the event aid and rescue is needed, which is most of the time, neither side can get to the other.

Until the "compact, impassioned mass" is either disbanded or finds reason, the prostitution of intelligence remains high treason against the "cause" of black advancement and empowerment. Treason against the millions of black Americans past and present who I'm sure did not take the lash, separation, dogs, water hoses, and more, so that we could fight among ourselves over degrees of blackness.

We may take divergent paths, make varying choices, have assorted destinies, but we all begin from the same point and, ultimately, will reach the same end.

Derrick Z. Jackson

BOSTON GLOBE

The Mark
of the Beast

African-Americans go into the twenty-first century wearing the mark of the beast. America's collective denial of racism has regressed to the point where this nation, built on the enslavement of black people, has made African-Americans its most prominent symbols of bigotry.

The case of Khalid Abdul Muhammad is most illustrative. In November 1993, Muhammad, a representative of the Nation of Islam and its leader, Louis Farrakhan, issued a squalid string of pejorative adjectives, calling Jews "bloodsuckers" and the Pope a "cracker." He also called for the killing of crippled and "faggot" white South Africans and ridiculed African-Americans he viewed as traitorous, branding Spike Lee "Spook Lee," for his unflattering portrayal of NOI founder Elijah Muhammad.

The public castigation of Muhammad's remarks would have been fair in a fair America. As it turned out, the vigor with which America condemned him revealed how uncommitted this country actually is to purging itself of the original sin of racism. Muhammad was one in a string of African-American men held up in recent years before the klieg lights of public opinion—Jesse Jackson, Louis Farrakhan, Leonard Jeffries, the rap group Public

Enemy, Sister Souljah, and Tony Martin—for words and writings that were, or allegedly were, tinged with hate.

The U.S. Senate was so outraged over what Muhammad said that it voted 97–0 to condemn his remarks, which it termed "false, anti-Semitic, racist, divisive, repugnant, and a disservice to all Americans." A *New York Times* editorial called on African-Americans in leadership positions to "renounce, root and branch Mr. Farrakhan's anti-white, anti-Semitic, anti-Catholic, anti-gay message." The editorial pages of the newspaper at which I work, the *Boston Globe*, had a similar tone:

- "Black leaders face a difficult enough task trying to secure social justice without the hate-filled baggage Farrakhan brings with him."
- "Should the [Anti-Defamation League] continue its campaign against anyone who tolerates the Muslims' anti-Semitism or backpedal a bit? Farrakhan's remarks show that such an uncompromising stance is the only defensible course of action."
- "If he [Farrakhan] does not quickly denounce anti-Semitism and all other forms of bigotry, he will be admitting that beneath that starched-shirt respectability of these men lurks an ideology full of hate."

Newspapers give plenty of space to African-Americans who speak out against African-American anti-Semitism. The *New York Times* gave Harvard University professor Henry Louis Gates its entire op-ed page one day in 1992. But no newspaper in recent memory has given its entire op-ed page to a critique of white racism.

On the political level, if Muhammad's words before a hundred or so students at Kean College in New Jersey were worthy of a Senate rebuke, then so too surely were the remarks of Sen. Ernest Fritz Hollings. A Democrat from South Carolina, Hollings, said, right around the time that Muhammad made his ill-fated remarks, that the reason "potentates" from African nations attended an international trade conference in Geneva was to assure themselves of a "good square meal" instead of "eating each other."

Calling black men cannibals goes back to the most primitive of stereotypes, ones which, in European eyes, made Africans a heathen race that needed Christianity—through slavery. But despite Hollings's track record of reported racial insults such as "darkies" and "wetbacks," the Senate gave him a college frat chuckle. His remarks were not viewed as false, racist, divisive, repugnant, and a disservice to all Americans. Jim Sasser, a Democrat from Tennessee, called Hollings's remarks "an inadvertence."

Jesse Jackson thought "Hymietown" was inadvertent, too.

When Muhammad called Jews "bloodsuckers," that was rightfully seen as uncivil discourse. But there was no hint of Senate outrage when Sen. Jesse Helms, the Republican from North Carolina, beat black challenger Harvey Gantt in 1990 with a TV ad that showed a white hand crumpling up a job rejection slip saying Gantt supported affirmative action, which obviously continues to suck the job market dry for white applicants. Instead, former Missouri Sen. Thomas Eagleton wrote in a guest column in the *St. Louis Post Dispatch*:

> *We know he [Helms] intended to fire up the white community by using an emotional issue as the spark to ignite the fire. But isn't Jesse Helms allowed the right to discuss an important and current national issue?*

While white America focuses on the falseness of African-American musings about Jewish involvement in slavery and pressures African-Americans not to be excited by the emotional speeches of Farrakhan, it, by its collective lack of outrage, gives Helms permission to excite white people against affirmative action, even though the attack is predicated on its own false theories of victimization.

There are virtually no statistics, particularly in the private sector, that show either where affirmative action has raised the percentage of African-Americans in the workplace to more than just half of our 13 percent of the national population, or where white Americans have been the least deprived. Even in the public sector, where affirmative action has enjoyed its best "success," many urban public school systems, while often 80 percent African-American and Latino in student population, remain majority white in teachers.

While many of the people arrested for crime in cities are African-American, most police forces remain predominantly white. Even the National Basketball Association, the entity in which African-Americans are 80 percent of the players, operates with a plantation mentality in which 80 percent of the coaches are white. African-Americans make up 20 percent of males in the military and 30 percent of service women, but among officers, we are only 6 and 12 percent, respectively.

Despite the 1968 Kerner Commission report and two and a half decades of liberal editorials exhorting the rest of society to live up to equal opportunity, and despite wide publicity given to the awful things happening in inner cities, newspaper reporting ranks are only 6.2 percent African-American. Management is only 3.1 percent African-American.

None of that factors into the collective white mind-set when sane discourse is needed. While white America now knows its African-American bigots on a first-name basis, the average citizen cannot cough up the name of a single skinhead, even though skinheads killed twenty-two people between 1990 and 1993. While the Republican Party can proudly claim it disowned David Duke, an easy task since the Ku Klux Klan is a worldwide embarrassment to the United States, the nation silently lets future Dukes get their education from white-supremacist cable-TV shows. One fellow, Herbert Poinsett of Tampa, said serial killers are white because "blacks don't have the brains to be serial killers."

When Klanwatch said white supremacist groups grew from 273 to 346 from 1991 to 1992, the Georgia Bureau of Investigation laughed it off as merely a reflection of power-hungry individuals who splintered off to start their own groups. Funny, white people did not laugh when Muhammad gave his remarks.

In Boston, such white denial allowed a confirmed enemy of African-American integration into the public schools and public housing, city councilor James Kelly, to creep all the way up the ladder to City Council president. Kelly's record of paranoid insensitivity included blaming proponents of busing as promoting "racial violence" and "a racial war" in the 1970s.

Right after winning the presidency, Kelly, who opposed integration of public housing in South Boston as recently as 1990, drew a classic separatist line in the sand in a *Globe* interview. He said if a black man wanted to date his daughter, "Then that would be a problem to me. . . . People, I think, ought to be left alone to live lives as they see fit. They ought to be free to associate with whom they wish and not associate with whom they wish not to associate with."

Flip this around for a second. What would be the outcry if Farrakhan had said, "If a Jew or any other white person wanted to date my daughter . . ."

But Kelly's animus was coddled by a majority of his fellow politicians, who felt none of the pressure African-American "leaders" get to distance themselves from Farrakhan. Mayor Thomas Menino went so far as to rewrite history to support Kelly for the presidency.

Menino said, "There is no harder working city councilor than Jimmy Kelly. When Jimmy Kelly was anti-busing, 99 percent of the city was against busing." Besides the idea that the term "99 percent" demeans the African-American children who ducked rocks hurled at the buses, Menino suggests that just because many people were filled with hate, it makes Kelly less accountable for his own demagoguery.

Menino did precisely what editorials demand that "black leaders" must not do: cut a bigot of his own color any slack, no matter what other work he or she has done.

The *Globe* published six editorials over a year-and-a-half period from 1992 to 1994 that focused on anti-Semitic statements or writings by African-Americans Farrakhan, Wellesley College professor Tony Martin, and Leonard Jeffries, the chairman of black studies at City College of New York. Yet it published no such editorials in 1990 when gubernatorial candidate John Silber issued remarks that were every bit as inflammatory as Farrakhan's. Silber said that based on his family experience, "The racism of the Jews is quite phenomenal."

The *Globe* did publish an editorial critical of Silber when the Boston University president wondered out loud if Cambodian immigrants were flocking to Lowell only to seek welfare. But such statements were not the central focus of any editorials determining his fitness to be governor. Hence, while the *New York Times* demands that African-Americans in leadership positions "renounce, root and branch" Farrakhan's brand of bigotry, and while the *Globe* supports the ADL's "uncompromising stance" against the same, white figures like Hollings and Helms and Silber and Kelly were allowed to bathe in hateful words without challenge from these same newspapers.

I should be clear and say that the *Globe* also deserves serious credit. I have published all of the above criticisms of my own newspaper in my column, with no pressure to change or adjust my opinion, at a time when several African-American columnists have lost or been threatened with the loss of their columns. The freedom to directly challenge the mind-set of a major newspaper is no small matter.

The mark of the beast on African-Americans is equally as evident in the debate on crime. The most dangerous signal came not from Presidents Ronald Reagan and George Bush, who clearly put civil rights in the obstructed view seats. It came from a man 86 percent of African-Americans put their trust in, President Bill Clinton.

Clinton had already matched Bush in the black-man-as-symbol-of-crime sweepstakes, tying Bush's Willie Horton TV ad with a momentary halt of his presidential campaign to return home to Arkansas to oversee the execution of Rickey Ray Rector, a brain-damaged African-American cop killer. But late in 1993, Clinton placed the mark squarely on all African-Americans with a speech that came from the pulpit of the same Memphis church in which Martin Luther King, Jr., gave his last speech the night before he was assassinated.

King said then that he had seen the promised land. Clinton spoke as if African-Americans had full run of the promised land for the last 25 years, after a combined 350 years of slavery and segregated disadvantage in America. Saying, "We gave people the freedom to succeed," Clinton told his church audience that King would feel betrayed by black-on-black violence in which "millions abuse that freedom to kill each other with reckless abandonment."

Afterward, Clinton was applauded and hugged by many of the African-Americans who crowded into the church to hear him. They applauded because, yes, violence is a terrible problem in many African-American urban neighborhoods. But also because the terror of that violence is so intense, many in the audience missed Clinton's profound lie.

No one "gave" us anything. What progress we have, black people fought and died for. As for "freedom," Clinton knows that African-American job applicants with the same résumé are rejected three times more than white applicants. Clinton did not say that African-American men who play by the rules and graduate college make only 79 cents for every dollar earned by white college graduates.

The reason Clinton left all this out of his Memphis speech was because his words were not intended for African-Americans at all. The speech (he gave a similar exhortation to Latinos soon afterward) was meant for the six o'clock news to give white America more proof that African-Americans are the metaphor for all that is wrong with our national character.

Clinton did not say he would stop his own violence. He fired first-strike missiles into Iraq. While decrying African-Americans' "reckless abandonment," Clinton runs the planet's most deadly developed nation, with a gun for four out of every five people. Clinton's White House is Earth's top pusher of arms to developing nations. Clinton has not gone to white churches to ask the CIA or the CEOs of Lockheed, General Electric, and Smith & Wesson to seek moral values and stop their reckless production of the instruments that destroy life.

Thus, Clinton maintains the momentum on Capitol Hill where "black" crimes of drive-by shootings and carjackings, and "black" drugs like crack, are attacked with lock-'em-up, death-penalty urgency, while 80 percent of murders happen between intimates of the same race, and white Americans consume 80 percent of illegal drugs

No president or candidate has said Jeffrey Dahmer, the LAPD, David Koresh, Charles Stuart, Howard Stern, or heavy metal lyrics represent the "reckless abandonment" of white morals.

Clinton will not deliver this multicultural, multivalent vision because the deck is being cleared of poor African-Americans to make way for the "white underclass." In a *Wall Street Journal* essay, Charles Murray, a fellow at the conservative American Enterprise Institute, said this underclass, fueled by "illegitimate" births, will have the same issues as low-income African-Americans, including violence.

"American society as a whole could survive when illegitimacy became an epidemic within a comparatively small ethnic minority. It cannot survive the same epidemic among whites. Doing something about it . . . should be at the top" of the "American policy agenda," Murray wrote.

Translated, African-Americans can kill themselves. White Americans must be saved. Clinton's speech on African-American violence, absent any charge to white Americans to take responsibility for their violence, has the net effect of placing society's mark of the beast solely on African-Americans.

The question then becomes, what do African-Americans in leadership positions do about the mark of the beast? Unfortunately, there are some signs that they may get sucked into the vortex, making African-Americans look worse than need be. Jesse Jackson has said, "This is the most self-destructive, life-threatening generation we've known . . . We lose more lives to drugs and guns annually than we have to the Klan in our entire history." And "If you come [to school] and you don't study, you have pulled the trigger on Malcolm, Martin, and Medgar."

Jackson has gone so far as to say today's African-American violence is "the new frontier of the civil rights struggle." But this obscures a full deck of history in which crime has held a high, haunting place for African-American elites. Also obscured is the history that the harder many elites work toward values, pride, and critical thinking, the more our government works to crush them.

In 1899, W. E. B. Du Bois said that even though racist conditions could excuse crime, "The amount of crime that can without doubt rightly be laid at the door of the Philadelphia Negro is large and is a menace to civilized people." In 1906, Booker T. Washington, whom W. E. B. Du Bois detested for accommodating segregation, said, "The worst enemies of the Negro race are those who commit crimes."

Their efforts at self-help were rewarded by lynchings in the South, race riots in the North, and the racial putdown of the movie, *Birth of a Nation.*

Marcus Garvey, well ahead of the 1990s' cry that black men are an endangered species, said in 1924, "The Negro is dying out. . . . There is only one thing to save the Negro, and that is an immediate realization of his own responsibilities."

But Garvey also pushed economic development with his Universal Negro Improvement Association. A young Justice Department officer, J. Edgar Hoover, labeled Garvey "the foremost radical among his race." Hoover worked to pin a crime on Garvey to put him "once and for all" out of commission. Garvey was imprisoned for mail fraud, then deported.

Hoover watched every African-American political figure, from Du Bois, to King, to the Black Panthers. His goal, according to Kenneth O'Reilly's book *Racial Matters: The FBI's Secret File on Black America*, was to "prevent the rise of a messiah . . . who could unify and electrify the militant black nationalist movement, and keep black activists bickering among themselves and to focus white America's attention on the inherently un-American nature of black protest."

In other words, Hoover was trying to keep African-American leadership from having, as singer-activist Paul Robeson said in 1958, "a single-minded dedication to their people's welfare. . . . Dedication to the Negro people's welfare is one side of a coin: the other side is independence."

The ultimate question of whether leaders of today should repeat the rhetoric of yesterday is whether any of it has to do with the general welfare of African-Americans and the rights we seek. For all the dreams of Jackson's drugs-guns/KKK line, the number of African-American homicides and drug deaths is only one-tenth the deaths from cigarettes and alcohol. Tobacco and liquor companies have gotten away with placing the mark of the beast on inner-city African-Americans precisely because they have purchased the silence of elite African-Americans with charitable contributions and scholarship programs.

African-American leadership must attack its demons. It must attack demonic speech so as not to lose the moral high ground in the war on racism as well as crime, because the only alternative is more death and more prisons. We must make critical moral decisions of our own because history shows that collectively white people will be of little help.

African-American leadership must also be clear on the current realities in a society in which most African-Americans, in the short term at least, will have to seek their employment from white sources. Troubled teens will exchange crack for calculus only when they see a legitimate economic carrot to go with the moralistic stick. That means fighting racism as never before. No matter how much traditional African-American groups may join white-owned newspapers in rebuking a Farrakhan, young people will continue to be curious about his cult, because the Nation's existence is precisely a reaction to the racism that continues to plague this nation.

African-Americans must be very careful in their response to bearing the mark of the beast. Booker T. Washington, three years before his death and after a career of hoping that a solid demonstration of African-American values and work productivity would alone bust down the walls of racism, had to conclude, "The Negro in the South has not had . . . a square deal" in education, and "from an economic point of view, the Negro in the North, when compared with the white man, does not have a fair chance."

It is clear that when the deal is square and the chance is fair, that is when you will see the violence stop. That is when you will see hate speech stop. W. E. B. Du Bois began this century by saying the problem would be that of the color line.

The intensity with which white people have maintained the line, from Willie Horton to *The Bell Curve*, from welfare queens to quota queens, and from prison cells to the war on affirmative action, ensures that it will divide us well into the next century.

5

The Ballot, the Bullet,
and Other Alternatives

Allegra Bennett

THE WASHINGTON TIMES

Black Labels

Conservative is not the best name to be called if you are a Negro. The word stirs emotions deep within the souls of most black folks who fear banishment from the race and condemnation as an unauthentic colored person.

While the conservative tag buckles the knees of many a black person with a supposed atypical black view, it is beloved by black political proselytizers who make their living trafficking in emotional hyperbole. Conservative becomes a handy little invective for those who think they have a lifetime lease on the thought of the whole black race.

Among such folk, a popular offensive is to draw a parallel between so-called conservative thought and the institution of slavery. It is the one way to keep atavistic views circulating unchallenged while suppressing fresh ideas. Black folks are no more a monolith than the Irish. Yet we are the only group in America saddled with race leaders, speaking for us as if we are a tribe of some sort. Truth be told, blacks harbor a plethora of ideas and what's interesting is that a greater number are traditionally conservative in outlook, socially and fiscally.

Many have very trenchant observations to share about the

pains of living black in America. But when those ideas are at odds with the liberal orthodoxy, out come the labels, hurled like rotten fruit at a bad act at the Apollo. Political types love the predictable clashes. But real people, who are most of America beyond the Beltway, keep their opinions to themselves. No one speaks for them in power centers like Washington, a town like no other that not only rejects the unfamiliar message but makes a sacrifice of the messenger. The irony is that conservative approaches—I'll do it despite the shackles—are what helped many blacks make the difficult transition from bondage to freedom. A firm belief in real self-help, education, and hard work as the keys to success are long-held tenets black folks have touted, labels notwithstanding.

As a writer practicing punditry publicly in Washington, I've been variously identified as conservative and liberal and conservative again. I enjoy the puzzlement, but I must say I'm especially taken aback to be called conservative. The Reagan years made *conservative* a four-letter word. Jerry Falwell, Pat Buchanan, and the Republican right wing defined it and gave it its rapier, mean-spirited edge. Their stridency left me with a cold, hollow feeling in the pit of my stomach.

But then, neither am I liberal, conservatism's evil twin. However, in a place as label-dependent as Washington, what you think you are means nothing. It is what other people think you are that controls, and folks must fit into neat, predictable categories.

The unfortunate result is that in the persuasion market achieving a consensus of ideas will never happen. If you have been assigned a label, you can have the wisdom of Solomon, but you might as well be in a roomful of the hearing impaired. Be a black woman with views that stray from the liberal spiel and the absence of sound is even more deafening, the level of paternalism cloying and palpable.

I first heard myself described as conservative about ten years ago when I was a commentator on a national television news magazine program that focused on issues of interest to black Americans. My real job was with a newspaper generally accepted as liberal in its view. So I suppose a liberal view is what was expected of me.

My journalistic colleagues on the set included one strident paternalistic liberal and an equally strident black conservative (an extremely rare breed then) who seemed to have trouble accepting that slavery was bad for black folks. Neither was playing with a full deck in my view. My liberal cohort believed that government was responsible for the hard times black folks couldn't seem to shake and therefore owed them a living in perpetuity. The designated conservative fumed that the welfare system dug into the pockets of hardworking people such as himself and should be completely dismantled as soon as possible.

Our on-camera clashes made for entertaining television but did nothing to advance the ideas of those of us who cleave neither to the traditional liberal posture people seemed conditioned to expect of blacks nor the aberrational posture some blacks in the limelight seem to take for the sake of controversy and a continued place in the limelight.

I observed that welfare had been bad for black Americans in the long run, since its paternalism broke up families and created a virtually intractable tradition of dependency where a tradition of self-help used to be and ought to be restored. Welfare as we knew it had to go. I naively thought that my views came down squarely on the side of common sense and defied the limitations of political branding. But you would have thought I was advocating genocide. The designated liberal responded first. He reached into his bag of predictable comments and accused me of blaming the victim.

I became defensive. But when I thought about it later I realized he was right. I was blaming the victim. But it was not necessarily a bad thing. When I have felt victimized the only way I could regain control was by figuring out exactly how I became a victim in the first place. When people can discover what led to their exploitation and passivity and identify the contributory role they are playing in its perpetuation, they have tapped in to power central. Reaching those answers critically and honestly is where victimization ends and self-determination begins.

That is the message I would have left him with if I'd had my wits about me. But I missed the moment. Name-calling is an old game among black folks. But when you recognize the cyclical relationship we have had with conservatives, liberals, Democrats, and Republicans you recognize the danger in labels. They work to keep a person firmly entrenched in a political, geographic, and mental ghetto.

More than anything, black folks need to become hard-core realist and challenge the status quo of ideas, whether they bear a liberal or conservative label. If any of us are to effect meaningful change in this life it has to come through the dynamic of thought. And that is discouraged. Most folks are not forced to defend their views. They simply gravitate to the company of people with similar thinking, largely avoiding confrontation.

Within a cocoon of affirming voices, much that is horse pucky slides by unchallenged, unsubstantiated. The I-know-what-you-mean grunt, smile, or nod frees most folks from any obligation to fully articulate a compelling position. Hence, we all get pretty flabby in the convincing arguments department, and at the first sign of debate we end up intimidated into silence for fear we will be stigmatized with a label.

Black folks must undergo a radical change in the way we think about ourselves as a race—no longer as the victims of 130 years ago who are owed something, but rather as extraordinary survivors who take life's lemons and make the tastiest lemonade in the neighborhood. We are in no position to do that when others are out there reenforcing the belief that someone else owes us the juice squeezer, the pitcher, and the sugar. They've already supplied the lemons. It's up to the beneficiaries to plant a seed and grow their own lemon trees. Now there's an idea that's neither radical nor belongs to conservative or liberal thought. It's survival. It's common sense.

Enjoy the Gas

Allegra Bennett

Driving along North Avenue, the unexpected tomato-red plaque momentarily flickers past your peripheral vision and the image sticks in your mind for several blocks. Tiffany Square is the legend printed on the provocative sign. It is affixed to a light pole just beneath the dark green guidepost with the white border that signifies the location's official name—Rosedale Street. The vast majority of Baltimore's streets are identified by green signposts, except for the brown ones the city put up in the late 1970s to distinguish the few areas anointed for urban gentrification. Tomato-red signs are rare. There is quite a story behind this one, one that symbolizes rotting humanity.

Tiffany Square juts out from busy North Avenue and stretches along two blocks of Rosedale Street coming to an end at the head of a little patch of grass in a busy intersection at Bloomingdale Road. The fertile garden that was planted there in August 1991 might produce bright red and pink perennials again next summer. Residents named the street and planted the patch in an exercise that was as much a catharsis for the neighborhood as a pathetic memorial to Tiffany Smith, a second-grader who lived in a house a few yards away until she was caught in the crossfire of two assholes who stood on opposite ends of the block where she played, shooting at each other in a battle over turf.

The small garden also stands as a reminder of a cruel, escalating urban holocaust. Especially difficult is knowing that the destruction harbors no tenderness for children, not Tiffany, who was six when she was killed July 9, 1991, not three-year-old Shanika "Nik Nik" Days who that August died on her father's lap when the three bullets pumped into his back passed into her, not ten-year-old Taurius Johnson who was ambushed while playing football in the street, and not four-year-old Quantae Johnson who was struck by a stray bullet that careened into his grandmother's house.

The violent death of innocents is particularly horrifying. Such acts evoke a spontaneous sob from somewhere down deep inside of me. "Something has got to be done about this violence" is the doleful refrain. But little happens. There's only the next sickening murder of a child or passerby, more acting out with candlelight vigils, slogan-ladened placards bending in the breeze, and more hollow pronouncements by vapid politicians who seem to miss the point that there already are laws on the books to deal with crime. It's just that the laws are compromised by consideration of all kinds of ridiculous extenuating circumstances that mitigate punishment into oblivion. Still, there are the rallies and the crowds and the television cameras. So cue the speech about how "We must strengthen the laws to see to it that . . ." blah, blah blah blah blah.

Weak or nonexistent statutes are not the problem. A society too timid to urge punishment that fits the crime is the problem. And our reticence is at our own peril.

Leave reprisal up to the authorities and nothing as final as what happened to these children will ever happen to their killers. Some killers need to be executed. Jeffrey Dahmer murdered seventeen young men in Milwaukee. There is no mistake about his guilt. He said he did it. What is it about his life that makes it more important than those of the people he cannibalized? John Thanos is on death row in Maryland. Once again, a question of guilt is not an issue. He did it. His comments on the murders of two of his three victims is astonishing. "If I could bring those brats back right now from their graves," he told the court during sentencing, "I would do it so that I could murder them again before their eyes, as they cringe in fear and horror, reliving this eternal nightmare." Gas him.

Opponents of capital punishment might advocate a sentence of life with no opportunity for parole in lieu of execution. But that's not enough. With every wretched murder that goes unpunished in kind, another layer of our humanity is stripped away. The sound of gunfire rips through neighborhoods daily. People hardly wince anymore. Gunfire seems to be accepted as a requisite sound effect of urban living. How long will it be before the murder of a child or the cold, calculated drive-by shooting of multiple victims elicit more than the sound of folks sucking air through their teeth? Justice and the spineless way it is practiced offers criminal minds no disincentives for carrying out their violent acts. They can get away with murder and they know it all too well.

Take the horrendous killing of Pamela Basu, whose car was hijacked by two car thieves in Howard County, Maryland. The thirty-four-year-old research chemist was dragged for nearly two miles to her death after she was forced from her car in front of her home. When the incident was first reported, television cameras at the scene panned to the gutter and focused on a dark mass that was indistinguishable at first. Then came the horror of recognition. The dark mass was the woman's hair, which was yanked from her scalp as she was dragged along the street.

Defense attorneys argued that the defendants, Rodney Eugene Solomon, 27, and Bernard Eric Miller, 16, did not intend to kill the woman. They were just after her car. What did they think she was trying to convey when she was screaming in horror in their faces? What did they think would happen to a person who is scraped across concrete at 40 miles an hour? What did they think would happen to the woman's fragile human body when they ran her BMW into the curb in an attempt to knock her loose from the car? Would she just get up and complain of a headache? What's more, Mrs. Basu's 22-month-old daughter was in the backseat. But not for long. Solomon said that the baby's crying got on his nerves. His solution? He threw the child out on the road, still fastened in her car seat. Did he think the baby would bounce? Fortunately, the child was not injured. If she had been, would his lawyers argue that he didn't mean to hurt her, he just wanted to shut her up?

Equally galling was the way the two attempted to manipulate the system. As a 16-year-old, Miller was not exposed to the death penalty and Maryland's gas chamber even though he was charged as an adult with murder. This, he knew. He flip-flopped about who was actually behind the wheel, even making the preposterous suggestion that both of them were driving at the same time. The public was supposed to envision each taking turns sitting on the other's lap while steering the car. Any reasonable mind would suffer no conflicting thoughts in this mockery. The fact is both men were complicit in Mrs. Basu's death. Pair them up in the chamber and invite them to enjoy the gas.

Unfortunately, they won't be inhaling poisoned air. Solomon's attorneys dished up mitigating circumstances of his background of poverty, ignorance, and drug use, as good defense attorneys are expected to do. The jury bought it. So instead of having their heads, we get rationalizations about what screwed up their heads: backgrounds of poverty, abuse as a child, ingrown toenails, a whole litany of irrelevancies why it is excusable to murder a child, a mother, a grandmother, anybody, over drugs, turf, a car, profit, barbecue.

Insolent punks who are more ambitious in their criminal enterprise than Mrs. Basu's killers cavalierly contend that jail time and death on the street are the costs of doing business that they accept in their line of work, as if that understanding gives their line of work nobility. They are rigidly clear about this. If only the judicial system were as focused and resolute about enforcing the penalties for violating the rules of order. State-conducted execution needs to be added to the balance sheet as yet another cost. When Solomon and Miller were sentenced to life terms, decent society shed yet another layer of its humanity.

Sometimes youngsters at play unintentionally offer clever insight into what they think of the world. There's a popular gag where kids make up an outrageous story and then with great exaggeration yell "Psyche!" when it appears their listeners have been sufficiently suckered in. To me the gag is a lampoon of adults who condition children early to ignore parental threats. How many times have kids heard Mom or Dad declare: "Do that again and I'll kill you." Criminal justice is proving about as menacing as those parents. It's a system of empty threats. So many exceptions are allowed such as to render the rule meaningless. Folks are getting away with murder.

I never thought I would come around to this way of thinking. Not long ago I felt that capital punishment was cruel and unusual and those who advocated it were as bad as cold-blooded killers. I harbored the specific fear that blacks would fall victim to execution more than others. You cannot live black in America and not feel a little paranoid about your expendability. But whether the head in the sand is black or white we are fooling ourselves if we think letting people get away with murder has no long-term consequence on the rest of us. It does. Sooner or later we all forfeit something of value—either our lives or our humanity.

Evidence is in that we now are paying dearly with both.

That which separates humans from the lower order of animals is becoming a difference with few distinctions—Dahmer; Joel Rifkin who murdered 17 prostitutes; John Wayne Gacy who murdered 33 men and boys, 27 bodies found in and under his suburban Chicago home; Arthur J. Shawcross who killed 11 women in Rochester, New York; a 16-year-old Baltimore boy who blasted two relatives to death, one a 77-year-old woman, because they kicked him out of the house. What is the magic number that triggers society's intolerance? What murder will be so atrocious that it provokes useful outrage? America already has the shameful distinction of being the most violent country in the industrialized world. We are suffering from an erosion of scruples and are conceiving a generation of babies who enter the world in the crosshairs of decaying morality.

Children are being conditioned by both the criminals on the street and a criminal justice system that lets predators get away with murder. Killing is no more offensive than spitting on the sidewalk. They both make you wince. But in time you'll get over it. Maybe the spitting, but I never want to get used to murder. I want to maintain that part of my humanity that makes me weep spontaneously and sincerely as I often do over reports of the carnage that now defines everyday life. Instead of futures filled with optimism and wonder, ten year olds engage in a macabre discussion among themselves, planning their own funerals. Twelve year olds carry guns to school "for protection" against other twelve year olds. This is utter madness.

We need to exercise the death penalty. Start with those blatantly obvious cases. That might persuade the next generation, if not the present, that life is a national treasure. Life, damn it, matters. Young folks spend an enormous amount of time in front of the tube. Interrupt "Beavis and Butthead." Televise the executions. Draw the nexus between behavior and consequence. Show them some real shit. Naming streets and planting gardens as a memorial to little children killed in the street war games is eviscerating. We have a death penalty. We need to use it.

Richard Prince

ROCHESTER DEMOCRAT AND CHRONICLE

The First Amendment Is Not the Enemy

In May 1993, a federal jury awarded $400,000 to Leonard Jeffries of City College of New York, saying the school violated his free-speech rights by removing him as chairman of its black studies department.

The outspoken Jeffries had been vilified after a rambling speech in which he implicated "rich Jews" in the slave trade and accused Jews and Italians of engaging in a "conspiracy, planned and plotted and programmed out of Hollywood" to cause "the destruction of black people."

Jeffries's reaction to the jury award: "I think the message is clear that there is freedom of speech, that that umbrella stretches to African people."

The same month, *Rolling Stone* magazine carried an interview with the rapper Ice-T, whose song "Cop Killer" was the center of a firestorm that eventually resulted in the song being pulled from its album. Asked what he had learned from the experience, Ice-T said, "I totally lost any belief in the Constitution, belief in the First Amendment. I totally changed my whole concept on this legal system."

The difference between Jeffries's and Ice-T's takes on the First

Amendment illustrates the ambivalence that African-Americans feel toward that pillar of our civil liberties.

Here in the mid-1990s, the feeling that "free speech" has become a little too free has seen black college students destroying campus newspapers they deem to be racist. So-called "gangsta rap" pollutes the airwaves with obscene depictions of gang life that reduce women to "bitches" and "ho's" and their male African-American peers to suitable targets for assault rifles. Ironically, this gangsta rap entertainment finds its greatest audience among young whites and makes fortunes for moguls of white-owned music companies, who ardently defend these rappers' "freedom of speech."

Well-meaning university administrators, meanwhile, seeking to provide an atmosphere of relative comfort for the students of color many of them began recruiting only recently, impose "speech codes" that attempt to ban "hate speech" from campus discourse. This has produced a backlash among white males who see themselves as victims of "political correctness." The anti-PC forces, insisting on their right to offend, cite the First Amendment. Julianne Malveaux, an African-American columnist, rejoins, "Hate speech, tasteless (at best) T-shirts that stereotype people of color, and other pugnacious expressions of white supremacy are not free speech but racism hiding behind the First Amendment." In a further irony, more than a few of those prosecuted under these speech codes have been black. The First Amendment, many African-Americans conclude, is a white thing.

Wrong.

It's true that no African-Americans participated in the drafting of the First Amendment. In 1791, most were slaves.

Yet the principles articulated in the First Amendment have had a profound effect on African-Americans. And in turn, African-Americans have had a role in shaping the limits of the First Amendment.

I'm persuaded that if more of us knew that history, we'd eagerly claim the First Amendment as our own—just as we already claim the Civil War amendments that freed us from slavery. I'd also hope that we'd realize that, as with any right, the freedoms of speech, assembly, press, and the rest come with responsibilities. Some might call the use of these freedoms to do harm—to poison our collective values, for example—a necessary price we pay for them. I call it a betrayal of those who fought to liberate us in the first place.

Prince Whipple was one of them. He was the black man you see in the paintings of George Washington crossing the Delaware in 1776. Owned by Capt. William Whipple, Jr., of New Hampshire, one of Washington's bodyguards, Prince Whipple was emancipated during the Revolutionary War. In the fall of 1779, Whipple was one of twenty "Natives of Africa . . . born free" who petitioned the House and Council of New Hampshire to restore their freedom. The Declaration of Independence had special resonance for blacks, both slave and free. To them, it was a black thing.

Whipple and the others supplied the words that were missing from the Declaration. They argued in Portsmouth, New Hampshire, that "Freedom is an inherent right of the human Species, not to be surrendered, but by Consent, for the Sake of social Life; that private or public Tyranny and Slavery, are alike detestable to Minds conscious of the equal Dignity of human Nature. . . ."

In states that allowed blacks to file lawsuits, such as Massachusetts, blacks went to court for their freedom, with mixed results.

There was no First Amendment when African-Americans began petitioning the government for redress of grievances. Mum Bett, an ancestor of W. E. B. Du Bois, was one of the winners. A daughter of native Africans, Elizabeth Freeman, as she was known legally, was a slave in Massachusetts. One day her mistress took a heated kitchen shovel to Mum Bett's sister, and Mum Bett deflected the blow. Mum Bett "resented the insult and outrage," left the home, and refused to return. When the master of the house appealed to the law for her return, Mum Bett cited the "Bill o' Rights" she had heard gentlemen talking about over the table she had waited on. Didn't it say that all people were born free and equal?

A lawyer took her case, and in 1781 a jury set her free—establishing that the Bill of Rights, at least the Massachusetts version, had abolished slavery.

Fittingly, a proposed black Revolutionary War Memorial recently planned for the Washington Mall intends to honor not only those who actually fought in the war, but those like Mum Bett and Prince Whipple, who petitioned for their freedom. The First Amendment wasn't passed until ten years after Mum Bett won her court case.

It's a continuing source of embarrassment that so many who proclaim their First Amendment rights don't know what it actually says. It doesn't declare that society is obligated to provide a platform for any thought someone feels moved to express, as too many believe.

It does say: "Congress shall make no law respecting an establishment of religion, or prohibiting the free exercise thereof; or abridging the freedom of speech, or of the press; or the right of the people peaceably to assemble, and to petition the Government for a redress of grievances."

For more than a century, the word *Congress* in the First Amendment proved to be a hindrance to African-American aspirations. "Congress" shall make no law, it says, and in 1833 the Supreme Court affirmed that that meant the states could restrict First Amendment freedoms all they wished.

Thus, as abolitionists began to print anti-slavery literature, almost every southern state passed laws mandating punishment —often the death penalty—for anyone distributing literature "exciting to insurrection" or with "a tendency to produce discontent . . . among the free population . . . or insubordination among the slaves."

Any statement that slaves ought to be free was seen as tantamount to fomenting insurrection.

The effect of these laws reached beyond the borders of the states that passed them. In 1829, a free black man in Boston, David Walker, wrote in pamphlet form a stirring call for resistance called "David Walker's Appeal in Four Articles; Together with a Preamble, To the Coloured Citizens of the World But in Particular, And Very Expressly, To Those of the United States of America."

The unbridled militancy of "David Walker's Appeal" is thought to have inspired Nat Turner to lead an 1831 slave insurrection. The state of Georgia offered $1,000 to anyone who would kill Walker. The next year, 1830, he was found dead near the doorway of the shop where he sold old clothes in Boston. He was believed to have been poisoned.

It got worse. Once a new Fugitive Slave Law was passed in 1850, any African-American who spoke out, thereby making his whereabouts known, placed himself at risk. Legally, any slave owner could claim that the speaker was an escaped slave. The slave owner could lawfully insist that proceedings be brought to "return" the African-American to him.

Nevertheless, many African-Americans dared to continue to speak out; dared to continue to write.

Let's not forget the First Amendment right to "petition the government for a redress of grievances." The nation saw the most powerful use of that right come after the Emancipation Proclamation was issued, in 1863.

The proclamation had declared slaves free only in states still rebelling against the Union. Petitioners gathered nearly 400,000 signatures on petitions asking Congress for legislation to end slavery. The petitions worked. Congress passed the Thirteenth Amendment, declaring slavery unconstitutional.

Still, our struggle continued.

The Union's victory in the Civil War changed African-Americans' status in these United States, but it still did not mean that Bill of Rights protections applied to the individual states.

Even though the Fourteenth Amendment—making blacks citizens—became the law of the land, the courts ruled that that did not mean they had full First Amendment protections.

In 1871, a large group of blacks gathered in a Louisiana church for a political meeting. They were set upon by a large number of heavily armed whites, and in the melee more than a hundred blacks were killed. Eventually, more than a hundred whites were federally indicted for murder.

The case that resulted—*U.S.* v. *Cruikshank*—marked the earliest time the Supreme Court upheld the right to petition and assembly. But the ruling did nothing for African-Americans. In that same 1876 decision, the court threw out the indictments against the whites. Under Louisiana law, the African-Americans were committing a crime simply by gathering. Since the blacks' meeting was held to petition the state government, not the federal, in the justices' minds blacks' constitutional right to assemble did not apply. The Supreme Court would not extend the Bill of Rights to the states until 1925.

It was on friendlier territory that W. E. B. Du Bois chose to convene a group of 29 African-American men from 14 states that started what became known as "the Niagara Movement," a forerunner of the National Association for the Advancement of Colored People. They met in 1905 near Buffalo, New York, in Fort Erie, Canada. In his autobiography, Du Bois listed the group's first two principles as "freedom of speech and expression" and "an unfettered and unsubsidized press."

That was entirely in character. An irate Du Bois called the meeting after African-American journalist William Monroe Trotter had been arrested and sentenced to thirty days in jail for questioning Booker T. Washington on his accommodationist views at a public meeting. Du Bois had proposed the conference "to oppose firmly present methods of strangling honest criticism; to organize intelligent and honest Negroes; and to support organs of news and public opinion."

Du Bois, a journalist among his many roles, knew well the significant role the press had played in the African-American freedom struggle.

The first African-American newspaper, *Freedom's Journal*, was published in New York City in 1827 by John B. Russworm and Samuel E. Cornish. A weekly, it was designed to answer attacks on blacks by a white New York newspaper whose publisher encouraged slavery.

The abolitionist press became a vital part of the struggle waged by Frederick Douglass and his white abolitionist colleagues. After the Civil War, it continued to crusade against such injustices to the race such as lynching, poll taxes, and other Jim Crow laws. In May 1892, the presses of the *Memphis Free Speech*, a black-owned newspaper, were destroyed after editor Ida B. Wells audaciously wrote that "Nobody in this section of the country believes the old threadbare lie that Negro men rape white women. If Southern white men are not careful they will over-reach themselves and public sentiment will have a reaction and a conclusion will be reached which will be very damaging to the moral reputation of their women."

Wells was out of town at the time and did not return.

The black press wasn't threatened only by irate local towns-people. During World War II, its publishers were challenged by the president of the United States. The black press had toned down its cries against racial injustices during World War I in order to help the war effort. When the black press was not re-warded with the elimination of those injustices, its editors and publishers felt they had been duped. Thus, when World War II arrived, injustice in the military became a prime target of black press outrage. There were no blacks in the Marines or Coast Guard as World War II began; African-Americans were turned away when they tried to sign up. There were no black Army Air Corps commissioned pilots. In the Navy, African-Americans could only be mess boys.

President Franklin Roosevelt sent his attorney general, Francis Biddle, to meet with *Chicago Defender* publisher John Sengstacke in June 1942. If black newspapers' tone didn't change, Biddle told Sengstacke, he was "going to shut them all up" for being seditious under the Espionage Act, which made it illegal to write or say anything that hurt the government's ability to prosecute the war.

As Patrick Washburn reported in his book *A Question of Sedition*, Sengstacke pointed out that black papers had been fighting racial prejudice for more than one hundred years; they were not going to stop now. "You have the power to close us down, so if you want to close us, go ahead and attempt it," Sengstacke told Biddle.

The standoff ended with a compromise, with black publishers agreeing not to become any more critical than they already were, and Biddle pledging that the black press would be granted inter-views with top government officials that were previously denied them. Still, FBI director J. Edgar Hoover tried until 1945 to obtain Espionage Act indictments of the black press. Fortunately, the Justice Department would not go along with him.

A generation later, the civil rights movement would furnish the Supreme Court with a case that redefined the First Amendment for modern times. *New York Times* v. *Sullivan*, decided in 1964, held that public officials could not be libeled unless it was proved that the statement was made with "actual malice." It was considered a stunning decision with profound implications for free speech, removing the threat that libel posed to the expression of ideas that angered those in power. The case began with a full-page ad published in the *New York Times* on March 29, 1960, signed by the "Committee to Defend Martin Luther King and the Struggle for Freedom in the South."

In addition to traditional civil rights figures, those who signed included entertainers Harry Belafonte, Marlon Brando, Diahann Carroll, Nat King Cole, Dorothy Dandridge, Ossie Davis, Sammy Davis, Jr., Ruby Dee, Eartha Kitt, Hope Lange, Sidney Poitier, and Shelley Winters. Baseball pioneer Jackie Robinson and former first lady Eleanor Roosevelt, among others, also signed this appeal to support the southern civil rights struggle, an appeal for rights as basic as the right of African-Americans to vote.

Though the advertisement named no names, a city commissioner of Montgomery, Alabama, named L. B. Sullivan claimed he was libeled by statements in the ad saying that southern officials had brutally suppressed peaceful protests. He sued the *Times* and four African-American ministers in Alabama listed in the ad for $500,000. An all-white jury awarded him the full amount. By the time the governor of Alabama and other officials joined the suit, the libel claims reached $3 million and threatened to intimidate the national press from covering the civil rights movement.

Justice William J. Brennan, Jr., wrote for the court: "The First Amendment, said Judge Learned Hand, 'presupposes that right conclusions are more likely to be gathered out of a multitude of tongues, than through any kind of authoritative selection. To many this is, and always will be, folly, but we have staked upon it our all.'

"Thus we consider this case against the background of a profound national commitment to the principle that debate on public issues should be uninhibited, robust, and wide-open, and that it may well include vehement, caustic, and sometimes unpleasantly sharp attacks on government and public officials."

The civil rights movement could not have proceeded without the unpleasantly sharp attacks from Martin Luther King, Jr., and Malcolm X. Nor could it go forward without African-Americans claiming their First Amendment freedoms to assemble, to petition the government, to speak—and to pursue their religion.

Since the days of slavery, religion has provided African-Americans with a survival mechanism. When every law, custom, and code of conduct was designed to reinforce the African-American's complete dehumanization, the knowledge that God had a different view of black worth became spiritually empowering. Religion provided underground leaders—the three largest slave revolts in American history were led by slave preachers—and the black church was second only to the black family as the preeminent institution in the African-American community.

At times, church gatherings were the only ones slaves were permitted to attend, and they became the context for planning insurrections and escapes.

The civil rights movement of the 1950s and 1960s, steeped in the black church, provided literally hundreds of court cases that tested the constitutional right to assemble and of free speech. One case came after the state of Alabama tried to retaliate against the NAACP, which in 1954 had won a lawsuit to force integration in Southern schools. The attorney general of Alabama filed suit to expel the NAACP from the state, and demanded that the organization produce all business records, including membership lists.

When the NAACP refused to produce the membership lists, the case went to the Supreme Court. The justices sided with the NAACP and established a constitutionally protected right of freedom of association.

As one indication of how many of our contemporaries have come to value such protections only when it suits them, we can look today to Texas.

Four decades after *NAACP* v. *Alabama*, a Ku Klux Klan group in Texas is being ordered to make public its membership list.

The Klan group is claiming the right of freedom of association and is being defended by an African-American lawyer. For his willingness to do so, lawyer Anthony Griffin was fired from his unpaid job as general counsel to the local NAACP.

Parade permits became another weapon in the arsenal of reactionary southern sheriffs, and the marches of the civil rights era thus led to courts to redefine the right to assemble. In 1963, the city of Birmingham, Alabama, denied parade permits to King, who wanted to lead protest marches from Good Friday to Easter Sunday.

King led the marches anyway. He was arrested and charged with parading without a permit and with violating a court injunction the city had obtained. When the case reached the Supreme Court in 1969, as *Shuttlesworth* v. *Birmingham*, the justices struck down the city's parade-permit ordinance as vague, saying it was obvious that the denial was based solely on who was going to parade and the subject of the marches. And that was an unconstitutional violation of assembly and free speech, the court ruled.

Laws tailor-made to harass particular groups of African-Americans didn't end with the civil rights era. Nor did challenges to them. In the 1990s, the Supreme Court struck a blow for freedom of religion for all Americans when it took the case of a group of Afro-Caribbeans in Hialeah, Florida.

Their Santeria religion mixes Roman Catholicism with West African beliefs brought by slaves to the Caribbean, and it involves animal sacrifice. In the United States, Santeria is usually practiced underground, but in 1987, a Santeria priest announced a plan to open a church in the Miami suburb of Hialeah. The city responded with an ordinance banning animal sacrifice. The Supreme Court ruled for the Santerias, saying it was obvious the government was singling them out for persecution, and that that was unconstitutional.

What a bind we African-Americans find ourselves in. Without the First Amendment, King could not have delivered his "I Have a Dream" speech; Malcolm X could not have written his autobiography. We would have neither the poetry of Nobel laureate Toni Morrison nor the passionate legacy of crusading journalist Ida B. Wells.

Yet none of the people we've just discussed fought solely for the First Amendment. It was a package deal. We don't control many of the broadcast outlets, the newspapers, the publishing houses that enable others to pursue the First Amendment to their heart's delight. For African-Americans, the Constitution didn't become personal until the Thirteenth, Fourteenth, and Fifteenth amendments, which made us full citizens in the eyes of the law.

Then as now, we didn't just want free speech, we wanted freedom from racism.

And that includes racist speech. Isn't that government policy, too, we ask? Equal protection of the laws? Tolerance? Inclusion? Can we in fact advocate both free speech and freedom from racist speech?

The history of the late 1980s and early 1990s isn't promising. On one side we have African-American parents fighting to remove Mark Twain's *Huckleberry Finn* from schoolrooms because of the novel's references to "Nigger Jim." The efforts have met with mixed success.

In Kansas City, Missouri, an African-American councilman, Emmanuel Cleaver, now mayor, fought to ban the Ku Klux Klan from staging "Klansas City Kable" on the public access channel. "I don't think we can sit passively and watch people who would like us to be dead receive a prominent spot on television," he said. The council first voted to remove the public access channel completely, then reversed itself.

In Chicago, African-American councilmen physically removed a painting that demeaned the late Mayor Harold Washington, Chicago's first African-American chief executive, from the School of the Art Institute of Chicago. The council members won.

In New York City, a coalition of African-American and Hispanic groups told the Federal Communications Commission it opposed granting publisher Rupert Murdoch a waiver so he could purchase the *New York Post*. The tabloid's history had been so racist, the groups said, that it was better to have no *Post* at all. The FCC granted Murdoch his waiver.

Two St. Louis disk jockeys used racial epithets over the air. The National Association of Black Journalists was quick to urge the FCC to take action. "The FCC continues to hide behind the weakened argument of freedom of speech to allow so-called shock radio to spew vicious racial slurs and veiled threats against African-American leaders," Sidmel Estes-Sumpter, president of the group, wrote to the FCC. "How long are we going to allow this kind of trash to permeate the airwaves?"

Meanwhile, members of an obscene and pornographic rap group named 2 Live Crew became the most visible African-American supporters of the First Amendment.

"This is a case between two ancient enemies: Anything Goes and Enough Already," a Fort Lauderdale judge wrote in finding a recording by the group obscene. He was overruled.

In 1994, the group was before the U.S. Supreme Court, carrying the banner for singer-songwriters who believe they have the right to parody a song and make money from it without the permission of the copyright owner. Who said standard bearers for freedoms had to be role models? Or even responsible?

Yes, some of us believe the First and the Fourteenth amendments can co-exist. But they are drowned out by others. As the "Kansas City Klan" case was being debated, an African-American councilwoman, a fifty-four-year-old grandmother named Joanne Collins, voted against pulling the plug on the public access channel. "I come from a philosophy that you learn by education and you don't withhold information," she said. "I have learned from even the most negative person, and because I don't agree with them doesn't mean that he shouldn't be heard, or that I shouldn't listen. I believe right will always prevail."

So many of her ancestors would agree with her. The shame is that so few of her contemporaries do.

Wiley Hall, 3d

EVENING SUN

The Myth of
Drug Wealth

Leon and I are sitting on his stoop in the 1300 block of N. Chester St. when a man rides by on a ten-speed bicycle.

"There you go," says Leon, nodding his head in the direction of the bicyclist.

"You think he's a drug dealer?" I ask.

Leon smiles grimly.

"What do YOU think?" he demands. "When else have you seen a great, big, grown-up looking man like that riding on a bicycle?"

The cyclist wears a silver and black sweat suit with the pants cut off at the knees. He has a heavy gold chain around his neck and a floppy hat on his head. He looks to be somewhere in his mid-twenties. Pumping smoothly, the cyclist turns the corner and disappears from view.

Leon says drug dealers in East Baltimore have started riding bicycles recently as a way of circumventing the city's anti-loitering law. The law was supposed to prevent pushers from congregating on street corners.

"But the drug dealers adjusted, like they always adjust," says

Leon angrily. "By riding a bicycle, they cover more ground. They cover it faster. And it's easier on their feet."

So, we sit here, Leon and I, pondering the almost mythical ability of drug dealers to outsmart the law, to evolve beyond the law's reach, to turn a profit off of every attempt to cut into their business.

"You think he makes a lot of money doing this?" I ask after a while.

"Of course he does," answers Leon authoritatively. "Man, the average dealer'll pull in a good $300 to $500 a day."

"That's almost $110,000 a year!"

"Damned right!"

"And you say he lives around here?"

"Most of the boys who deal drugs around here, also live around here," says Leon. "That's the tragedy. They are destroying their own communities."

"So," I ask then, "where does the money go?"

"What?"

"You're talking about a whole group of young men in this community who are pulling in over $100,000 a year," I note. "So where does all the money go? What do they spend it on? That guy on the bike doesn't look affluent to me. This doesn't look like a neighborhood where a whole bunch of people have vast amounts of disposable income. So where is it? Where's the money?"

"Hmm," says Leon. "I never thought about that."

Perhaps, it is time we *started* thinking about it—that, and a whole lot of popular assumptions surrounding our war on drugs.

We are made to believe that drug dealers bestride our communities like giants; that they represent the best and the brightest of black manhood; the potential entrepreneurs and leaders who turn to crime because they believe that all other avenues for success are blocked for them.

We are told that drug dealers outsmart and outgun our law enforcement officers.

And when it comes to recruiting the young, we are told that drug dealers can offer youngsters a better deal than that offered by traditional role models such as teachers and ministers; a life of excitement and wealth; a future that is tangible, that youngsters can see and touch and believe in.

Each of those perceptions has a consequence: when we complain that the "best and brightest" of our young men turn to the drug trade, we imply that those not involved in the trade are suckers, are less than bright. When the police say they are outgunned by the bad guys, we feel compelled to pour resources into new weaponry and equipment for them. And because we have become convinced that drug dealers can offer our young a better deal, many adults do not even try to compete.

But what if those assumptions are false? What if drug dealers aren't so smart? What if the apparent impotence of the police in this war on drugs can be traced to something other than a lack of firepower? And what if a career in the drug trade is not as attractive as it seems?

The Joint Center for Political and Economic Studies, a Washington-based think tank, reported recently that most street-level dealers are not striking it rich through the sale of illegal drugs as is popularly believed: "Less than 20 percent of the people engaged in drug dealing have a net cash return of as much as $1,000 a month. Less than 5 percent of all people who deal drugs have a cash income that allows them to purchase expensive cars."

Even when street-level dealers make decent incomes, the Joint Center found, most of them consume their profits by purchasing and using drugs themselves.

Says Katherine McFate, a research associate with the Joint Center: "These findings have important policy implications because they suggest that job training and employment programs could appear very attractive as alternatives to those in entry-level positions in the drug trade.

"The popular assumption is that young people are making so much money selling drugs that a job at McDonald's cannot begin to compete," continues McFate. "But what if they are not all making that kind of money? What if, in the corporate-style gang organizations the large sums made from dealing drugs are not trickling down to the lower echelons?"

This strikes me as an important issue—maybe even a central issue.

Some experts estimate that as many as one out of five black urban teens is connected in some way to the drug trade. Yet, the neighborhoods where the trade flourishes—and where these kids live—remain the poorest in the city.

Where are the record shops? Where are the thriving sportswear stores, the automobile dealers, furniture emporiums, and fine jewelry shops? Where is there *any* evidence in *any* of these communities that 20 percent of the young people there have suddenly acquired vast amounts of disposable incomes? Most of those kids still live in apparent poverty. Businesses in those neighborhoods continue to die.

Can any community absorb millions of dollars a year without leaving a trace?

Where does the money go?

"You raise a good point," says Lt. Owen Sweeney, a shift commander for Baltimore's Eastern District police station, when I put my questions to him.

"The people we arrest for dealing drugs don't have a lot of money—at least, not to spend on themselves. They are wearing the same clothes as the working stiffs, they live in the same neighborhoods. And the big cars are not as prevalent as people think. The big profits must be going up the chain, because you're not seeing them enjoying the fruits of their labor."

None of this comes as a big surprise to the people who live closest to the drug trade.

The Chester Street corridor is described by police as the site of one of the major drug markets in the city. It is a community of row house apartments, liquor stores, corner groceries, and storefront churches. Abandoned buildings and vacant lots interrupt the block like missing teeth. Trash that clutters the curbs blows up the street on windy days. Schoolchildren must wind their way through clumps of slump-shouldered addicts and the hard-eyed young men who supply the drugs.

The Chester Street corridor is as devoid of affluence as a community can be.

"There ain't no rich people around here," says the manager of Joe's Cut-Rate Liquors at Chester and Federal Streets. Yet, he estimates that two-thirds of the young men who frequent his store are connected in some way to drugs.

"They ain't got no money," notes the manager. "Nobody around here's got any money."

"So where does it go?" I ask.

"Where it always goes, I guess," he answers. "It goes back to the Man. To New York. To Florida. To the 'burbs. It goes right back to the top."

Katherine Brady is selling dresses, smocks, and children's clothes from a little table in front of her row house in the 1300 block of N. Chester Street.

"If people around here are dealing drugs, they're taking their money someplace else, because they sure aren't spending it around here. You don't see any new cars around here. People aren't buying their places. You might see a lot of kids with those expensive shoes on, but that doesn't mean anything because a lot of times their parents buy it for them."

Othar Jones, who has owned and operated Jones' Barbershop on Chester Street for twenty-seven years, adds: "The ones we lose [to the drug trade] are the young men. They are the ones who give up, who go after that big drug money. But, now that you mention it, you're right. The kids who're dealing drugs never seem to have any more money than the ones who're working. I know them all. I cut everybody's hair. A lot of times, the dealers'll have less money on them."

"So why do so many kids get into it?" I ask.

" 'Cause they don't know no better," says Jones. " 'Cause they're too stupid to look around and see what's really happening and there's nobody around to point this out to them."

Once you sweep aside the myths, it becomes clear that the drug trade is *not* an attractive career option for young men. It offers a life with few rewards, constant violence, and continual police harassment. Between 1988 and 1992, more than 3.5 million people have been arrested for drug offenses nationwide according to the U.S. Justice Department, and they are serving longer sentences than ever before. Over that same period, thousands of young men in Baltimore alone have been killed or crippled as a result of drug-related violence.

Yet when our young people weigh their career options, many conclude that their future lies in dealing drugs. Prison, maiming, or early death apparently looks better to them than the alternative: a quiet life of hard work, sacrifice, money in the bank. Talk to young people, in fact, and many aren't even aware that there *is* an alternative.

All of this tells me that there is something tragically wrong with the way we are conducting our war against drugs.

Gregory Stanford

MILWAUKEE JOURNAL SENTINEL

A Crusade for
Our Children

On a sunshiny day in 1963, the civil rights train came rumbling into Washington, D.C. Fueled by sweat and blood and courage, the protest special had been chugging through the South, crashing through barriers into forbidden, perilous terrain. My daddy's cousins came down from New York City to greet the train, the talk of the nation, and we joined him. There I was, shoulder to shoulder with my heroes, freedom fighters fresh from southern battlefields. Somehow the ground underfoot seemed hallow.

The March on Washington brimmed with optimism, as did much of the civil rights movement. True, the southern campaign had many scary moments, and casualties. Still, the momentum seemed to lie with the anti-apartheid warriors. Justice *will* at last run down like waters, and righteousness like a mighty stream. All the civil rights crusaders had to do was to "keep on pushing," as the Impressions put it.

Boy, were we naive. The train, of course, derailed far short of its destination: racial justice. And the movement isn't back on track yet.

The march streamed from the Washington Monument to the Lincoln Memorial, where Martin Luther King, Jr., delivered his famous "I Have a Dream" speech in which he noted that a check given to the Negro and drawn on the bank of justice had come back stamped "insufficient funds."

King is long dead. His followers say gamely that you can kill the dreamer, but you can't kill the dream. Over much of black America, though, hovers what may be the stench of a dead dream. Witness the frequency of gunshots and out-of-wedlock births, the once lively night spots stilled by fear of crime, the massive pullout of public and private resources, the dearth of a movement to improve the black plight. King's dream no longer seems to animate much of black America.

Yes, some African-Americans did gain as a result of the opportunities the civil rights movement opened. But the masses fell further behind. On the eve of Ronald Reagan's revolution, poverty fighters and others warned that if the federal government were to withdraw services to the poor, the consequences would be dire. Well, the feds withdrew services to the poor; the consequences were more dire than what was forewarned.

An economic trend, the downturn in manufacturing, contributed to the worsening plight of African-Americans, who, as the last hired at the factories, were the first let go. On the forefront of this trend was my new hometown, Milwaukee, which is about as blue-collar as cities come. Here and elsewhere black workers didn't fare as well as laid-off whites in switching to service jobs.

Where is Rosa Parks when we need her again?

Local law and custom required her to give up her bus seat to a white man, but she refused, thus sparking the civil rights movement. That was December 1, 1955, in Montgomery, Alabama. Today black America desperately needs a second spark, a second movement.

The new crusade should depart significantly from the earlier version in that it ought not to be aimed primarily at white America. Sure, in this interconnected nation it's hard to ignore white people. They do control jobs and the capital needed to get ahead. But the civil rights train derailed as a result of a mighty collision with white resistance, which seems not to have softened one whit since. So the new crusade should try a different route.

Yes, control over wages, health care, investments, media images and the like lies mostly outside of black America. But one resource lies entirely within our community: our children. They are the rightful focus of the movement that must be. We must reclaim our kids.

"I have a dream," King said as the throng roared approval, "that one day down in Alabama, with it vicious racists, with its governor having his lips dripping with the words of interposition and nullification, one day right there in Alabama, little black boys and black girls will be able to join hands with little white boys and girls as sisters and brothers."

Three years later King tried to get little black children to live side by side with little white children. He took the civil rights crusade north, to Chicago, where he pushed open housing. The white response came as a rain of rocks and cherry bombs, prompting King to remark that not even in the southern campaign had he seen such hatred and resistance. So long as it stuck to tackling Jim Crow in the South, the movement enjoyed white support in the North. The Chicago campaign transgressed the parameters.

Viewed narrowly, the civil rights movement dissipated because it had achieved its goal: the eradication of Jim Crow. "Colored" and "White" signs came down in the South. Both blacks and whites could now eat at the same lunch counters. Congress and the courts outlawed discrimination in housing, in voting, in employment. This state of affairs, in fact, has led some conservatives to declare that race matters no more. No longer does black skin hold a person back or white skin push him ahead, they say. His people have reached the Promised Land that King espied from the mountaintop.

However, Jim Crow was merely a surface manifestation of an inequality that runs so deep it's entwined in the very foundation of this nation. The broader mission of the civil rights movement was to root out this deeper problem and thus effectuate genuine equality of opportunity between blacks and whites. The movement fizzled before it could fulfill that mission. Thus, while blacks can now drink from the same water fountain as whites, this nation remains in essence racially unfair. In other words, King's people are still wandering in the desert.

Our youngsters know this truth—but as a rule only instinctively, not intellectually. Rage particularly fills the hearts of our young men. They sense they are not getting a fair shake in life. They are supposed to serve as providers, a role that joblessness often keeps them from playing. The problem isn't the rage, which under the circumstances is normal. The problem is what they do with the rage. They aim it at one another or their girlfriends or innocent bystanders, rather than at its source.

"Gangsta rap" mirrors this problem. Yes, as defenders of the genre note, this art does imitate life—but too well. The lyrics thus repeat the mistake young people are making in life: misplacing the anger. Hence, women are ho's and bitches, with just one reason for existing. And the N-word often describes the other half. It's possible to reflect harsh reality and to transform it at the same time, à la folksinger Tracy Chapman, original rapper Gil Scott-Heron, and even songwriter-singer legend Marvin Gaye. (Check out his entire album, *What's Going On*.) In contrast, the gangsta rappers succumb to their surroundings and thus to the (racist) forces shaping their milieu.

Where, oh where, is Rosa Parks? Where is that spark to propel a movement?

The new crusade must salvage our young people. Yes, we African-American grown-ups lack enough jobs or enough wealth to go around. But, darn it, we can still have an impact. We must focus on the minds, on the brains of our youngsters. Specifically, we must see to it that their intellects are developed academically as much as possible. True, that's why we have schools. But obviously, for many black kids, schools aren't working. We must take matters into our own hands, and with the same intensity we displayed at the peak of the civil rights movement.

What form ought this new movement to take? Well, it should feature at least these three activities:

• **Tutoring.** This ought to be the new crusaders' chief thrust. Tutoring centers should sprout at least as much as churches do in black neighborhoods—in church basements, schools, community facilities, and private homes. Top priority must go to ensuring that every child is grounded in the three R's, but the effort mustn't stop there. Tutoring should include advanced subjects, too. Even then, though, the concentration must be on higher math and upper-level English, since mastery of those subjects leads to higher test scores and good grades in other subjects. The tutoring could evolve into reading or writing clubs for youngsters, who would select their reading materials with a little adult guidance or who would engage in writing projects with feedback from professional wordsmiths.

Tutoring is obviously work for Du Bois's "Talented Tenth"— African-American engineers, mathematicians, journalists, college professors, and others who have mastered the educational system. At the same time, the movement must engage regular folk. It doesn't take a college degree to teach the basics. Parents, especially, must become involved. Sessions could be held giving them tips on ways to make their children school-ready, and some parents could serve as tutors. Parents without the basics could use the occasion to go back to school, so they could better position themselves to help their children academically. Every African-American grown-up ought to feel responsible for playing some role in the tutoring campaign—even as simple a one as ensuring that their nieces and nephews are getting proper help. Every tutor need not be black; whites and others could serve in that capacity. But the black community, not outsiders, must shape the campaign.

• **Interaction with public schools.** The new crusade can't stick just to tutoring. It must interact with the present educational system, even though that often means reaching outside the black community. That outward thrust can't be helped; no way can you wage a massive tutoring campaign while ignoring the school system. At least coordination must take place between the system and the community. But at times the relationship may have to be confrontational—over, say, poor performance of a neighborhood school. The community may want the ouster of an incompetent principal or poor teachers. In such cases, politicking and old-fashioned protesting may be in order. The tutoring program should give the community moral leverage in battles with the educational establishment.

• **The start-up of new schools.** The movement may want to

run schools of its own. Since schools consume a lot of energy and money, this course should be undertaken only after hard and careful analysis. But this drastic measure will conceivably on occasion be the best prescription. Private schools must have a sound financial mechanism that doesn't keep out poor kids. A new educational concept—charter schools—may be a better answer. The community could get a charter to run a public school, and without the red tape of personnel rules that befog traditional public education. The trouble is, in most localities, this concept is just that; it's not yet law. Pushing for such a law would be a worthwhile cause, which would entail taking on powerful teacher unions.

We must undertake this new children-oriented crusade clear-eyed. We mustn't lose perspective. As crucial as education is, it's really not the most pressing issue African-Americans face; lack of jobs is more pressing. Were blacks right now simply to fare as well economically as whites with identical educational levels, a good deal of our troubles would be over. The corollary is that more education won't by itself bring about racial parity.

Still, we must make a crusade of education. In that sphere we can have impact by ourselves, with minimal contact with whites. And our efforts should narrow the racial gap.

To be sure, the lack of support from the larger society will handicap the struggle. Consider that a big reason education is such a hard sell for many youngsters is that they don't see much good coming from it. The older kids who do graduate seem to wind up at best with dead-end jobs that don't pay well. If the larger society were to pour decent jobs into the black neighborhoods, school would make more sense to young people, and our education crusade would gain momentum faster. But in no way can we count on that sort of help. Time and again since the 1980s, the larger society has made it abundantly clear that it would sooner build more prisons than create more jobs to solve the "black problem." So we have no choice but to go it alone.

Still, our isolation will make the challenge of launching a new movement all the more awesome. We must convince African-

American kids education pays without being able to guarantee them the most tangible payoff: jobs. Here are three lines of argument we would probably want to employ:

- The more education you have, the more income you have. No, chances are you won't have as much income as a white man with the same amount of education. But that's reason for you to get more education than he has. While you may know high school grads who aren't doing well, your own chances of succeeding do rise with education.
- Education will become even more paramount in the high-tech information age, which has already dawned. No longer can a worker muscle his way into a decent standard of living; he must have skills. While an education doesn't guarantee a job, a lack of education these days virtually guarantees poverty.
- Education is a valuable, albeit intangible, asset that white America really does not want you to have. So getting an education is an act of rebellion. There are other payoffs besides jobs. Developing the mind exposes you to liberating ideas, enables you to think better and to communicate more precisely. It enhances your personal power, which you could, in turn, employ in behalf of the African-American struggle.

The new crusade need not mean that black people should ease what pressure they might be applying to white America. It's okay to keep pursuing, for instance, diversity in the workplace and fair treatment in housing. It's just that the primary focus must be inward, not outward.

Likewise, the concentration on education need not preclude other self-help initiatives. In fact, one such initiative, the start-up of businesses, would nicely complement an education crusade. A proliferation of business enterprises would mean jobs for newly educated young people.

For strategic reasons the next African-American mass movement must focus inward. But the United States is too interdependent for that stage to last forever. Some day we must redeem that promissory note at the bank of justice—a goal that will likely entail a head-on confrontation with white America. Right now, though, we are not ready for that day of reckoning. An interim movement, focused on saving black kids, will give black America new strength, better preparing the community for that awesome day. But that's a future essay.

Meanwhile, onward with the children's crusade, which needs a modern-day Rosa Parks to ignite it.

Sometimes there's no accounting for the twists and turns in the course of human events. Seamstress Parks was by no means the first Montgomery Negro to be arrested for failure to relinquish a bus seat to a white person. Heck, Montgomery wasn't the first southern setting for a bus boycott protesting segregation laws. But somehow, in the wake of Parks's arrest, the chain of events and the cast of characters clicked just right to set into motion a movement that sent the American caste system topsy-turvy.

When will such a propitious moment come again? That, of course, is impossible to predict. Surely helping to give the Montgomery events momentum was the gifted leadership of Martin Luther King, Jr. But keep in mind that the boycott itself was the end result of a history. Before King there was Vernon Johns, who, preaching about justice, prepared the way for the drum major, much as John the Baptist tilled the soil for Jesus. Notably, Montgomery boasted an active chapter of the National Association for the Advancement of Colored People, as well as an active Negro women's organization, the Women's Political Council. And the city was home to an experienced black labor organizer, E. D. Nixon.

The point is that Montgomery's black community was ready. Sure, much about the boycott was spontaneous. But it simply would not have taken place without the civil rights infrastructure that existed in the city at the time. Parks herself was the local NAACP's secretary. And while her arrest wasn't planned, local Negro leaders had been on the lookout for a court case to test the transit segregation laws.

In like manner, African-Americans today must get ready. Nobody knows where the next spark will strike, but it needs tinder to keep burning. Rather than idly wait for a Parks or a King, we must actively put pieces of a tutorial infrastructure in place. A commitment to tutor just one child would be a handsome piece.

If only we persevere, a new Rosa Parks, a new Martin Luther King, Jr., will emerge. And, goodness gracious, a new locomotive will come tearing through the nation, transforming it as it goes.

Michael Paul Williams

RICHMOND TIMES-DISPATCH

Substance Over Style

I watched with joy, pride, and hope on the sun-kissed January afternoon that L. Douglas Wilder was sworn in as the nation's first elected black governor.

That night, as Governor Wilder and his daughter waltzed during his star-studded inaugural ball, Camelot appeared to have shifted from Cape Cod to the former capital of the confederacy.

"WE DID IT FIRST IN VIRGINIA" the black-and-white bumper stickers boasted. The smug tone of the message masked the unspoken wonder of it all; if the grandson of former slaves can be elected governor of Virginia, anything is possible.

But four years later, as Wilder prepares to leave office, the optimism of that gorgeous day seemed foolishly naive.

In Virginia, the aptly named Old Dominion, governors cannot serve two consecutive terms. That distinction appears to be the only thing stopping state voters from drumming Wilder out of office.

A poll conducted shortly before Virginia was to elect a new governor showed Wilder with an unfavorable rating of 53 percent—worse than televangelist Pat Robertson, scandal-prone Sen. Charles S. Robb, and fumbling President Bill Clinton. Similarly poor showings in a poll several months earlier left at least one pundit suggesting that the governor was not being judged fairly.

"The low approval rating of Wilder is almost entirely unrelated to anything of substance," said Dr. Robert Holsworth, a political science professor at Virginia Commonwealth University. "It's the style and the atmosphere of this governor, much more than the substance."

Style vs. substance. Instinct vs. intellect.

For so long, African-Americans have been cursed by the stereotype that we're all style and no substance.

We've been told we make great athletes and entertainers—both, of course, requiring little more than God-given foot speed, hang time, and natural rhythm. "It's like I came dribbling out of my mother's womb," Isiah Thomas once complained of the media's emphasis on the "natural" abilities of the black athlete.

That stereotype isn't confined to the athletic arena.

Jesse Jackson has flair and the gift of gab. But the skeptics write him off as all talk, lacking in experience or accomplishment. Even after he negotiated the freedom of a downed American flyer in Syria in 1984, Jackson couldn't shake that knock.

Style over substance.

As a career politician who'd climbed through his state's political hierarchy, Wilder stood in stark contrast to Jackson—to the point that the media fueled a rivalry between the men.

But oddly enough, the double-edged curse would inflict upon Wilder the unkindest cut of all: a failure of style.

In a state that prides itself on fiscal conservatism, Wilder should have gone out a hero. His tight-fisted, no-new-taxes approach to the budget helped maintain AAA bond ratings despite the recession and defense cuts in military-heavy Virginia. For two consecutive years, Virginia was rated as the best-managed state by *Financial World* magazine.

Any CEO's primary job is to keep his finances in order in good times and bad. Wilder was up to the task.

Wilder's four-year term included other substantial accomplishments. He won a nationally recognized victory over the powerful National Rifle Association by pushing through a law that prohibited the purchase of more than one handgun per month.

Another crowning achievement was his hosting of the 1993 summit between the Southern Governors Association and the leaders of nearly thirty African nations. The Richmond summit —largely ignored by the national media—resulted in a trade agreement between the southern states and the African nations.

But Wilder, it appears, was undone by a style that was alternately charming, abrasive, and in-your-face confrontational.

Much of America still likes its black heroes smiling, humble, and grateful. But Wilder's political career had been marked by calculated confrontation. His confidence, outspokenness, and I'm-in-charge assertiveness almost certainly was seen as arrogance by some of those who give him low marks.

The harmony and goodwill that marked his ground-breaking ascension dissipated almost immediately in a shower of spats with fellow Democrats. Wilder had to know he couldn't win those battles, but he wasn't one to turn the other cheek. For that, he was called petty and vindictive.

Critics complained that Wilder had the temerity to run for president when he should have been tending to state business. They complained of his frequent travels and jet-set tastes. And then there was his long-running "feud" with Sen. Charles Robb, in which Wilder always seemed to come out the loser.

Robb allegedly attended cocaine parties in Virginia Beach. A former beauty queen claimed to have had an affair with him; Robb only admitted she gave him a "massage." Robb's office held on to an illegal tape of a Wilder phone conversation, hoping to use it against the senator's political rival. When the hare-brained scheme backfired, Robb claimed ignorance and escaped indictment. Several of his staff members weren't so lucky. Still, Wilder was seen less as a victim than the heavy in the feud.

At times, Wilder suggested he was under more intense scrutiny because of his race. Practices that were overlooked in his predecessors' administrations were suddenly news. His relationship with Patricia Kluge, who is white, also certainly hurt him among blacks and whites. But at other times Wilder exhibited a tendency to play the race card to his own convenience, dealing a color-blind hand when it served him.

Under pressure to admit women to Virginia Military Institute, Wilder endorsed a plan that would create a military program at a nearby women's college—thus preserving an all-male VMI. This drew harsh criticism from some black leaders, who called it a reincarnation of the "separate but equal" doctrine employed during the segregation era. They accused him of selling his soul in an attempt not to alienate white voters he'd need to unseat Robb. Such was the balancing act of being a black governor in a predominantly white state.

Still, Wilder's greatest sin seems to be that he alienated people, even his allies. But being a nice guy guarantees nothing in politics. Ask David Dinkins.

Reputations for meanness didn't hurt Nixon or Johnson any more than being a nice guy helped Jimmy Carter. But black politicians still aren't judged on the same plane as their white counterparts. That's one lesson of the Wilder era.

Only a fool would count out Wilder, the quintessential political survivor. His legacy is already etched in stone. For whatever else is said about him, Doug Wilder was undeniably competent. And ultimately, we'll be better served by his triumph of substance over style.

Miki Turner

ORANGE COUNTY REGISTER

The Silence of Athletes

The common cold. Anticlimactic Super Bowls. Bell-bottoms. Darryl Strawberry's persistent on- and off-field dilemmas. Marge Schott. Racism in sports.

All things that, despite our best efforts by our best minds, just won't disappear.

You can eventually conquer the cold. Turn off your TV on Super Bowl Sunday. Choose not to wear those bells. Pray that you catch Strawberry on one of his better days. And hope that Schott, the would-be Nazi, will eventually get more than a slap on the wrist from Major League Baseball for her unrepentant ramblings.

Racism, however, sticks to us like pine tar on a bat.

In a perfect world it would appear that sports, the one arena that has the ability to bring people of different races and genders together, would be exempt from the world's ills. I guess that's a silly notion, though. A touchdown by Jerry Rice gives the 49ers a 50–0 lead and eliminates racism from the Super Bowl of life.

Not likely.

During the last couple of years, I've logged thousands of miles spending countless hours talking with athletes, team owners, managers, coaches, attorneys, sociologists, and fans about this ongoing problem. All agree that it's the most unpleasant aspect of their industry—other than free agentry. But none of the above could score any points when asked about possible solutions or remedies.

This did not surprise me.

Racism is far too complex an issue to be solved during a twenty-minute phone conversation or in between turns at the batting cage.

What I have learned, however, is that many of the wrong people—those on the outside of the game—are speaking out, while those on the inside remain silent.

External combustion is made more effective by internal flames.

In sports, those flames are the athletes. The same ones who thrill us with their gravity-defying dunks. Awe us with thunderous 400-foot grand slams. And bring us to our feet with their end zone antics after scoring the winning touchdown.

My criticism, however, doesn't apply to all. There are some bench-warmers who simply aren't in the position to speak out. They have a lot to lose, including their jobs. Conversely, high-profile athletes—like Sir Charles, Magic, Barry Bonds, and Warren Moon—who have that liberty, don't have to preach. Some injustices are so obvious that a simple sound bite will suffice.

Norman Lockman

WILMINGTON NEWS JOURNAL

Black and Brazen

It has never been easy to be black and brazen. A hundred years ago—even thirty years ago if you happened to live in the back swamps of Alabama and Mississippi—it could be deadly. Now it only marks you as a "militant." That is progress of a sort, I suppose, but it could also be that outspoken black people aren't taken as seriously as they once were. We still show our fangs, but white people aren't as fearful as they once were of the real poison in them. The more likely response is a kind of "how-dare-you" outrage.

The American Jewish community still tries to make Muslim minister Louis Farrakhan a bogeyman, but in the great scheme of things that fuss carries about as much relevance as the Federal Communications Commission's effort to take Howard Stern's raunchy radio personality seriously. Farrakhan may be infuriating to Jews, but he is basically harmless.

Actually, though, Farrakhan helps to make my point. There are more virulent strains of anti-Semitism being articulated than Farrakhan is accused of. Jews take these on, too, but Farrakhan is singled out for a particular brand of outrage for being black and brazen. So was Jesse Jackson when he made the "Hymietown" remark during his 1988 presidential campaign.

White people don't try to kill us anymore for being sharp-tongued and smart-mouthed (although they didn't mind seeing Malcolm X go down). More often they try to relegate our troublesome speech to the sidelines, as nothing more than stupid bad taste or racial goofiness; loudmouth street preaching or brainless rap. We do it so well they think we must be doing it for entertainment, theirs and ours. It is much easier to turn black brazenness into a fringe activity rather than give it serious treatment. This is particularly true when black brazenness attacks white shibboleths.

I was not greatly surprised the morning that Capitol Hill got its first dose of Surgeon General Joycelyn Elders. Sen. Ted Kennedy's Labor and Human Resources Committee has more than its share of liberals—Howard Metzenbaum of Ohio, Paul Simon of Illinois, Tom Harkin of Iowa, Barbara Mikulski of Maryland, and Teddy himself—but in the room that day they were just a kind of Greek chorus. Nobody paid much attention to them. Kennedy fussed and fumed over a conservative delaying tactic, but the real action came from the steaming outrage of the Republican mossbacks, Strom Thurman of South Carolina and Dan Coats of Indiana.

Senator Coats, the lackluster Republican who took over former Vice President Dan Quayle's old seat in the upper chamber, repeatedly tried to denigrate Elders's intelligence and judgment by challenging her comments about sex education, abortion, and condoms. (She's been misquoted and taken out of context too much for me to repeat all the accusatory lines again.) At one point he challenged her handling of affairs at a home for the elderly as though she were a nurse rather than a physician. As far as I was concerned, most of her questioned comments were simple straight talk. But Coats and Company were wild with outrage.

The purpose of this exercise was to put Dr. Elders in her place. The liberals played to the predominantly black gallery, but the conservatives played to what they hoped was the sentiment of the nation, excoriating her for her well-documented criticisms of attitudes and organizations, including the Catholic church. Senator Coats's job was to be highly affronted at the nerve of this big brazen black woman, trailing her M.D. and sitting before her large family, who had the gall to call into question the mores of the good white Christian majority. Dr. Elders looked more like a dressed-up version of the black women in some of these senators' kitchens than somebody who thought she should be the country's top doctor. Dr. Elders was missing a key ingredient: humility.

Capitol Hill had already dispensed with the "Quota Queen," Lani Guinier, whose academic musings were treated as though they were a direct contradiction of the Old and New Testaments. Now it was time to take on the "Condom Queen." Guinier had the nerve to criticize the integrity of some voting maps and laws, those sacristies of state's rights, and to suggest that there be draconian remedies. The liberal senators just took a dive on Guinier. They were scared to confront a black woman they thought was likely to talk back. So was President Bill Clinton. The potential for white outrage was too high.

Dr. Elders's back talk took their breath away. It even made some of the moderates squirm a little. She grinned and shuffled a bit at first, being super nice and trying not to sound too Arkansas, particularly as the liberals stroked her. But in the end, when the conservatives took off the gloves, she gave better than she took, without apology. It is the last thing a respectable black person is expected to do when publicly taken to task by a white person in a position of authority. When it was over, Sen. Nancy Kassebaum, the Kansas Republican who was more or less supportive, reprovingly advised her to improve her "bedside manner." By that she meant "learn to be more respectful to white folks."

Dr. Elders's problem was that she made Senator Coats sweat and squirm during his attacks on her. She was supposed to be the one to sweat and squirm. The fact that she did not was not appreciated by the Republican mossbacks and, out of pure spite, they made her wait a few extra months to be confirmed.

It is hardly a phenomenon for whites to expect blacks to be mealymouthed. Black people did not talk back to white people in the days of bondage. When they did, they found a medium for their expression that cloaked the real meaning, sometimes so thoroughly that they could mock the master to his face and have him slapping his knee and inviting his friends to come witness the blackface comedy. But straight talkers got the treatment, they were whipped into submission or, if they were truly incorrigible, they had their tongues cut out or their lips sewn shut and were left to die a slow death in the presence of their helpless loved ones.

There is, of course, a safer route for those of us who are black and driven to be outspoken. We can aim our most devastating salvos at black people. Nobody much minds that except other black people, but what can they do but grin and bear it? It is not at all unusual for black social critics (and that is what black columnists are—or should be) to win his or her spurs by proving that no barb will be spared on black folks. This is by no means a suggestion that black critics should be mealymouthed about black problems. It does suggest that we sometimes quail at the thought of bearing the slings and arrows that will inevitably fly our way when we dare criticize white mores from outside the refuge of our blackness, from the same ground as white social critics.

My black column-writing colleagues and I have drawers full of mail that calls us every kind of racist you can imagine because we criticize white icons, myths, and attitudes. We also have drawers full of mail praising us for our courage and candor. If you sort that mail carefully, you will find that most of the "courage and candor" encomiums are about columns that have taken on some black problem or taken black people to task. Mail from black people will often complain about "airing dirty laundry," or simply try to project blame back onto white people.

If I have excoriated some white behavior from a black point of view the mail turns nasty, but there is still a sense that I have stayed within my expected parameters, that I am speaking for "my constituency," as one anonymous wacko likes to call it. But if you want to see the truly aberrant mail, shuffle through the stuff that comes in from people who have read something in which I have commented critically or derisively on subjects dear to the hearts in Archie Bunker-land, not as a black writer but as an American.

I routinely call Rush Limbaugh "Rush Limberger." Just masking a passing reference to "Limberger," not devoting a whole column to him, which would be overkill, can generate a wave of name-calling that escalates into spheres of racial psychoses I have seldom witnessed. I once wrote a column suggesting that Oliver

North was a bounder and a cad, not worthy of a warm spit bath, not to mention a U.S. Senate seat or, heaven help us, the presidency (I also said he was so shallow that he would probably want Mr. Limberger to be his running mate), and for several weeks the mail poured in, most of it from the Midwest, upstate New York, and the South, where my column gets a lot of mileage. Many began with "How dare you . . ." and went downhill from there. I learned a lot of new derogatory names for black people in general and for myself in particular. My favorite was from a writer who called me "niger" throughout five handwritten and barely legible pages and said that the reason he was for North was because he would have the good sense to line up "nigers" and shoot them like the Germans did the Jews. I forwarded it to Ollie.

One of the strangest of the letter phenomena, though, was a sequence of mail I received from a reader in upstate New York who read a paper that carried my column without an accompanying photograph. At the time, I wrote several columns critical of Israeli policy toward Palestinians. The reader angrily suggested that I was a self-hating Jew (maybe the name fooled him), but nevertheless took the time to apprise me of my errant thinking. Some time later, I received in the interoffice mail a letter to my paper's editor from the same reader, with a column attached that had my picture with it. The column was not about Israel, but it was about the political shambles of the post–cold war Europe. The writer suggested "confidentially" that my column was a waste of space because it dealt with things that "this cultural cripple could not possibly fathom."

"Cultural cripple." Very descriptive. Very revealing. It is the nexus of the attitude that black people have no right to be critical about "white" subjects outside of a racial context.

The poor man probably didn't know the term, but my parents, prisoners of their era, used to talk disparagingly about black people who became "biggity." A black doctor in my rather white hometown (he was one of three resident doctors) once decided that it was time he lived up to his reputation for being wise, respected, and rich. Much of his practice was white. When one of the doctor's white colleagues decided to move from a large

Spanish-tiled villa with specialized office space, Doc decided he'd buy up. The house was no more than three blocks from his old house. It might as well have been in Palm Beach. No deal. The neighbors objected. Having saved all that money from being denied the house, our Doc then decided to join the local country club where many of his patients were members (though as far as I know he had never touched a golf club, couldn't swim, was too fat to play tennis, and wasn't particularly sociable). His application was accepted and sent into some kind of waiting-list black hole (no pun intended), where it remained until the day he died. Meanwhile white newcomers breezed into the club within weeks of their arrival.

My parents shook their heads (this was in the early 1950s) and murmured that Doc had gotten too biggity. It didn't matter that he could build a duplicate villa on property he owned on a street dominated by black people, it was biggity to try to buy that house on Cypress Street and join the country club. What's he going to do next, try to join the Episcopal Church?

Dr. Elders is biggity. Lani Guinier is biggity. I suppose I'm biggity. Jesse Jackson is not biggity because he works almost exclusively within the framework of blackness. Jesse Jackson is "militant." Supreme Court Justice Clarence Thomas is not biggity, because he proves he knows his place by slapping other black folks around. Colin Powell is not biggity because—pay attention here, this is critical—white people don't really consider him to be culturally black.

One of the main reasons some successful black people learn to stop being too culturally "black" is to avoid the "biggity" problem. It is a major contributor to the problem of the isolation of the black middle class from the black underclass. In certain carefully controlled settings it is possible in America to temporarily escape stereotypical blackness. "Temporarily" means as long as you can keep the great mass of blackness as far away as possible. You can do it by being a foreigner (sophisticated black people are constantly asked, "Where are you from?" the assumption being that you are not a black American). You can do it by being a black contrarian, like Justice Thomas, or by being invisible, tucked and rolled away in wealthy neighborhoods with carefully culled friends who are above the race, as long as nobody shows up at a party with screw-top wine.

The last thing in the world these latter folks want to do is be racially brazen. It blows the game. This does not mean you cannot be supportive of black causes and what I call "high black culture"—artists, musicians, artisans, and bygone heroes. As a matter of fact, this is an important part of the game, and part of the mystique. It is your cultural contribution to making white people in this milieu feel good about themselves and you. It does mean you cannot speak well of "vulgar" blackness or try to explain that some bad things that happen in black communities aren't just based on stupidity and debased personality traits.

This is what ripped Zora Neale Hurston from the bosom of the Harlem Renaissance. Even as an anthropologist with good reason to immerse herself in rural black culture to document it, she was perceived to be embracing it too warmly to satisfy her more assimilationist colleagues, who regularly trashed her for what they considered her glorification of niggerishness. It's something we have to get beyond. It won't be easy. Too many of us have escaped through the eye of the needle and when we look back we see only niggerishness, which spurs us to put even more distance between ourselves and our people. We work too hard at finding secret places to let down the pretenses and be ourselves. So do white people, I'm sure. Either way, it is most unhealthy and most unwise.

Every time I hear of a white colleague being bemused—and often deeply troubled—over why black people clump up together in cafeterias, college dormitories, even neighborhoods, I am reminded how difficult it is to explain in America the phenomenon of feeling OK about being black without apology.

It is no laughing matter in America to be black and to be willing, even momentarily, to publicly reject white standards and conventional wisdom. We all know that those who do are marginalized and, if possible, humiliated. It may be preferable to the whippings and death penalties for black brazenness in slavery time, but can nevertheless be a terrifying prospect.

Fear is such a part of black life in America, although it is often cloaked in bravado, that to contemplate being a serious critic of white life here can seem to be suicidal. Look at the evidence. Martin Luther King, Jr., lost the white mainstream (if he ever really had it while alive) when he expanded his agenda from a crusade against racial bigotry to stand against national involvement in the Vietnam War. Suddenly it was perceived that he had overstepped his bounds, not just by the segregationists whose hatred helped drive the bullet into his head, but by people who, because he was black and brazen, thought it was none of his business.

It is not easy to be black without apology in America—or anywhere else in the world where we are thought of as inferior beings. But learning to be black without apology is the threshold of true freedom. It is a goal infrequently attained, because it so often requires great internal and external struggles, but not a soul should doubt its value.

Photograph Credits

Lisa Baird: courtesy of Bergen County *Record*
Betty Bayé: courtesy of the *Louisville Courier Journal*
Allegra Bennett: courtesy of *The Washington Times*
Howard Bryant: courtesy of *Oakland Tribune*
    (photo by Tom Duncan)
Michael Cottman: courtesy of *New York Newsday*
Betty DeRamus: courtesy of *Detroit News*
Dorothy Gilliam: courtesy of *Washington Post*
Wiley Hall, 3d: courtesy of *Evening Sun*
Derrick Z. Jackson: courtesy of *Boston Globe*
Harold Jackson: courtesy of *Birmingham News*
Claude Lewis: courtesy of *Philadelphia Inquirer*
Dwight Lewis: courtesy of *The Tennessean*
    (photo by Robert Johnson)
Norman Lockman: courtesy of Wilmington *News Journal*
Deborah Mathis: courtesy of Tribune Media Service
Brenda Payton: courtesy of *Oakland Tribune*
Peggy Peterman: courtesy of Graham Photography
Richard Prince: courtesy of *Rochester Democrat and Chronicle*
Jeff Rivers: courtesy of *Hartford Courant*
Gregory Stanford: courtesy of *Milwaukee Journal Sentinel*
Miki Turner: courtesy of *Orange County Register*
    (photo by Nadia Borowski Scott)
Larry Whiteside: courtesy of *Boston Globe*
Michael Paul Williams: courtesy of *Richmond Times-Dispatch*
DeWayne Wickham: Ironlight Studios, Baltimore, Md.